Spirit Builders. It's A Process

First Edition

Dr. Irene Y. Bernard

Words2HelpBuildYou®

Welcome to the Process

This book is dedicated to all of the passionate counselors, devoted life coaches, and spiritual leaders that make the daily commitment to help people "go through and grow through" the processes of life.

Words2HelpBuildYou

Cordova, TN 38018-6661

1-901-878-2067

www.spiritbuildersinc.com

©2016 by Words2HelpBuildYou

First Edition

Printed in the United States of America

All scriptures quoted from the New Revised
Standard Version of the Bible. (NRSV)

Copyright Pending; case-1-3256488851

Library of Congress Control Number: 2016906631

Spirit Builders, Inc.

Spirit Builders: It's a Process

1. Admit – can't fix it if it ain't broke

2. Believe – Trust in the power of faith.

3. Challenge – The challenge of life & change

4. Differentiate – Enemy or inner-me?

5. Evaluate – Reflection time for self-evaluation.

6. Forgive - Let go and allow healing to take place.

7. Grow – Discover & cultivate the new you.

8. Honor – Self-care & nurture you.

9. Integrate – Combine & Start fresh.

10. Juxtapose –Pros and cons.

11. Kindle – Spark change with your story.

12. Love – Make the commitment to live, laugh, & love

Spirit Builders, Inc.

Prologue

Did you ever have an idea that was so big and so exciting, that it made your heart race when you thought about it? It was approximately fifth teen years ago that God planted such a seed in my heart. The seed of an idea for a simplified, self-help system that guides our understanding through a process for accomplishing a victorious life.

This is a labor of love, a process that God outlined through personal experiences, private testimonies, and the stories of those whose paths I've crossed along the way.

The theme is "Deliverance;" Deliverance as defined by living a life free from habits, guilt, hurt, anger, fear, and shame. Deliverance as it relates to restoration, liberation, and being made whole.

This is not a quick fix method to excel you through the process but a twelve stage strategy for a triumphant release. Do the work and the work will manifest in you.

Every week a different principle is introduced. Deliverance takes consecration and dedication. Start each day out with prayer. Read and pray concerning each daily affirmation. Reflect on the personal stories and accounts of those that have embraced the process. Journal how the process feels to you. Listen to the "Deliverance" CD often for inspiration and share this life altering experience with others.

Acknowledgements

To God, the only wise creator of all; I thank-you for patiently and consistently guiding me through this process called life. To my beloved pastor Dr. Lawrence Braggs, your ministry continues to stretch me in areas I never knew I was capable of growing. To the talented Rev. Darrell Petties. I've worked with many pastors and leaders but few compare to working with you. Thanks for your support.

Thanks to the many awesome and anointed men and women of God that so diligently serve in ministry, seminary, treatment centers, and schools, as intercessors, teachers, preachers, nurses, counselors, and more. Your work inspires me. Iron truly does sharpen iron. Thanks to each and every one of you for the gifts you are to The Body of Christ.

Thanks to two very important men in my life; my son (Dru) and my brother (Eduard), to my extended family Cheryl (mom), Jen, Mark & Jermaine' To Larry, Ruby and Shana, you guys caught the vision early and supported it from the start: and thanks to each of you.

Admit

Before we can truly move forward, we must become willing to be true to ourselves. This level of honesty shines a light on our character defects and they have robbed us from the truth of who we are.

The bible says the "truth shall make you free…" It does not say that fabrications, exaggerations, or falsehoods create freedom but that the hard, cold, and honest truth has the capability of restoring liberty to our lives.

This devotional is dedicated to the deliverance process. The first stage of any process is admitting that there is a need to enter or start the process. Admit where you are physically, spiritually, and emotionally. Admit who you are behind the scenes, without the bells and whistles. Admit what you have done, how you did it, who you did it with, and the motivation that made you do it all.

Admission can be a challenging experience, but it has to be done before moving forward. Each stage of the deliverance process is a building block for the next. Compromise on any stage of the process and the entire process will be compromised. If that happens, the entire process will eventually crumble and fall apart.

So prayerfully enter this first stage of the deliverance process and allow each story to help you make your own admission.

Day 1

For now, we see in a mirror, dimly, but then we will see face to face. Now I know only in part; then I will know fully, even as I have been fully known.

I Corinthian 13:12 NRSV

For nine years I thought I could pray hard enough to stop my husband from smoking crack. For nine years I would make excuses for him missing work, and skipping school. For nine very long, gruesome years, I thought that his sobriety was my responsibility.

No one could help me because no one ever knew what really was going on behind our closed doors. No one knew how many telephones and VCRs were replaced because Evan would need to supply his body with the demand that was being made on his soul. Nine very long years with my eyes glazed over and my faith full of so many holes that hope would just leak right through.

Suddenly, out of nowhere, things began to turn around for the better. It started as I looked out over our backyard watching Evan cut the lawn and I said these words out loud, "This man is an addict and there's nothing I can do about it." That was my turning point. The "Ah-Ha" moment that starting the healing process for me. The moment of admission.

Today I am ready to admit -

_____

_____

_____

_____

_____

_____

_____

_____

_____

_____

_____

_____

Day 2

Pride goes before destruction, and a haughty spirit before a fall.

Proverbs 16:18 NRSV

My husband left us ten years ago, during a time when I was a full-time student and homemaker and our daughter was having a difficult time in school. It was humiliating. We had become "some of those people" who "needed" government aid. Although, I refused to apply for it.

Months went by where we had little to no food. Then, out of the blue, an old friend I had not seen in over twenty years came by the house. She just so happened to work for the department of human services. She said it was my right as a tax paying citizen to apply for any aid I was illegible for. She preached, "This was why these programs were created." But I found it hard to admit that I had become "one of those people." I lost my husband, my child's father, and our livelihood and now I'm being asked to give up all I have left, my dignity.

Eventually, circumstances forced my hand and we quickly became "one of those people." I learned the truth of that statement as I stood in line at the DHS office. Life can happen to anyone. Who are any of us to criticize and judge others? Everyone has a story and some of our stories include a chapter on admitting we need help.

Today I am ready to admit -

_____

_____

_____

_____

_____

_____

_____

_____

_____

_____

_____

_____

Day 3

For God did not give us a spirit of cowardice, but rather a spirit of power and of love and of self-discipline

2 Timothy 1:7 NRSV

Carol was a successful, educated woman and everyone knew it. What they did not know, was how she lived in fear. Carol was afraid failing so she became a workaholic. She was afraid of gaining weight so she exercised excessively. She feared being ignorant, so she obsessively read books. For years Carol didn't understand that fear was controlling her choices throughout life. How could she? To the public Carol was an ideal.

Eventually, fear began to affect her physical health. The prognosis was an imbalanced Ph. System caused by stress. Her physician recommended that she de-stress immediately and suggested that Carol she a therapist to help her find ways to balance the stress in her life. It was in therapy that Carol learned that the attempt to control things had put undue stress on her body. Control was Carol's way of combating the unspoken, unrecognized fears that plagued her mind.

It wasn't easy for Carol to admit that she was afraid. Somehow it made her feel vulnerable and sometimes even more fearful. But, as she continued to admit her fears and the need to control, the stronger and more confidant she became.

Today I am ready to admit -

_____

_____

_____

_____

_____

_____

_____

_____

_____

_____

_____

_____

Day 4

The Pharisee, standing by himself, was praying thus, 'God, I thank you that I am not like other people: thieves, rogues, adulterers, or even like this tax collector... But the tax collector... was beating his breast and saying, 'God, be merciful to me, a sinner...for all who exalt themselves will be humbled..."

St. Luke 18:11, 13, 14 NRSV

"I never considered myself a drug addict, just a social drinker. Maybe I'd have a glass of wine (or two or three) after work, at parties, or with dinner, but an alcoholic I was not. I came to treatment to avoid going to jail on a DUI charge.

That was how I lied to myself for years until one day something clicked. I was sitting in a therapy group like we were made to do every day. However, this time something different happened. One of the ladies was sharing their story and I thought to myself, "There but for the grace of God goes I." But what did that mean? If God is no respect of person then God's grace was extended to everyone. I looked at my sister and realized, "There goes I."

I immediately admitted to my Higher Power, myself, and my peers that I was an alcoholic and addicted to pompous behavior. That revelation and admission saved my life and my mind and taught me to love and respect people today.

Today I am ready to admit -

_____

_____

_____

_____

_____

_____

_____

_____

_____

_____

_____

_____

_____

_____

Day 5

But God chose what is foolish in the world to shame the wise; God chose what is weak in the world to shame the strong;

1 Corinthians 1:27 NRSV

Over the years I've stuffed myself in too little body shapers, complained of a sluggish metabolism, and criticized smaller women for being underweight and unhealthy. I lived in a state of chronic denial. I refused to admit that I was lazy, greedy, and just plain ole' fat. My mind created a system that held me hostage but a small, loving child set me free.

I was in the mall when I saw a small boy slip and hit his head. His mom had both arms full so I rushed to his rescue. I helped him up and gave him a hug. He turned to this mom and as she was saying Thank-You, I overheard him say, "Mommy she's so soft and jiggly. I pushed out a smile and walked away with his words echoing in my mind, "soft and jiggly." It hit me like a rock. I couldn't lie to myself any longer, I'm fat. I'm soft, jiggly, and fat and I'm fat because I'm greedy and lazy.

Wow that really hurt but my young friend helped me to admit what I've spent years denying. Now I think before I eat, pre-plan what I'm going to eat, and move as often as I can. Today I can say I may still be soft but most of the jiggly is gone.

Today I am ready to admit -

_____

_____

_____

_____

_____

_____

_____

_____

_____

_____

_____

_____

Day 6

It has often cast him into the fire and into the water, to destroy him; but if you are able to do anything, have pity on us and help us." Jesus said to him, "If you are able —All things can be done for the one who believes." Immediately the father of the child cried out "I believe; help my unbelief!"

St. Mark 9: 22-24 NRSV

My big sister and I have lived together all of our lives. We made a promise to take care of each other no matter what life threw at us. Living with Brandy was an adventure. Some days she would be a fun-loving person and other days she would lie in bed and cry for hours. I thought that the best way to keep her happy was to get her what she wanted when she wanted it. I thought this would keep her in that fun-loving state of mind, but it never seemed to work.

One late night Brandy came into my room and grabbed me by my feet and literally drug me out of the house. I was so disoriented I thought I was in a nightmare. That night standing in the cold and rain with only my nightgown on, turned into a pivotal moment. We both had to admit that my sister had a problem. We needed professional help and that is exactly what we got. Calling the CMHD (The Center for Mental Health Disorders) was the second bravest decision we've ever made. The first was admitting that there was a problem. Today we are fine. Healing is coming to us both.

Today I am ready to admit -

_____

_____

_____

_____

_____

_____

_____

_____

_____

_____

_____

_____

Day 7

Serenity Prayer

*God grant me the serenity
to accept the things I cannot change;
courage to change the things I can;
and wisdom to know the difference.*

*Living one day at a time;
Enjoying one moment at a time;
Accepting hardships as the pathway to peace;
Taking, as He did, this sinful world
as it is, not as I would have it;
Trusting that He will make all things right
if I surrender to His Will;
That I may be reasonably happy in this life
and supremely happy with Him
Forever in the next.
Amen.*

Reinhold Niebuhr

Learning to admit that I had sacrificed a life of
serenity for confusion and chaos wasn't easy. I
considered myself a woman of peace. Now I realize
that much of the pain I suffered was self-inflicted. I
was a people-pleaser and love-seeker. I had to admit
that I tried to manipulate people into loving me and
doing things for me. Today I admit that I have
limited power and I use it to only help change me.
Today I change those things I can change and
accept those I can't and I am always praying to
know the difference.

Today I am ready to admit -

_____

_____

_____

_____

_____

_____

_____

_____

_____

_____

_____

_____

_____

Trust & Believe

Trust is a very intimate and fragile thing. Whether you trust too little or too much, it remains that trust is influenced by our past. Once trust is broken and hope destroyed our sense of safety becomes endangered. We feel insecure and may begin to question the level of honesty, motives, intentions, feelings, and actions of those around us. When we allow ourselves to trust another, we open our hearts to a level of vulnerability that also leaves us open to great pain. We acknowledge that we have confidence in the entity we put our trust in. This means we believe in the reliability of the resource to perform in a particular way. The problem occurs when those we trust disappoint us repeatedly.

We build walls around our hearts for protection from further hurt only to close ourselves off from the good things in life. Specific steps must be taken to repair the sacred bond of trust and help us to believe again. The next section is complete with stories of how some chose to work through their own trust issues.

Trust is the second empowering principle or tool that will help guide us through the processes of life. Learn to believe in something greater than you that loves and desire to help you and. Believe that you can make it through the process. Trust yourself and trust the process.

Today I trust that -

_____

_____

_____

_____

_____

_____

_____

_____

_____

_____

_____

_____

_____

Day 1

I can do all things through him who strengthens me.

Philippians 4:13NRSV

I was reading through an old journal and ran across an entry I made after a Sunday service. It appears that one of my favorite female evangelist was our speaker for that day. Apparently she shared a story concerning her health. In the circles I frequent, we call that a testimony. She spoke of feeling tired but thought nothing of it. She continued to travel and push past it until she just couldn't ignore it any longer. She went to a doctor and they ran tests. The results revealed an 80% blockage in the artery above her heart. Then she made a comment that cut through my existence today, "I was living on 20%."

I started looking through my old journals in search of something that would encourage me. Life had knocked me out and kicked me while I was down. Then I read, "I was living on 20%" and I began to believe again. Those words gave me a fresh perspective. Instead of focusing on the 80% and being reluctant and fearful. I decided that if she could live on 20% until things got better, so could I. I don't remember what her sermon was about but her testimony restored my faith and today I trust that the 20% will sustain me until…

Today I trust that -

_____

_____

_____

_____

_____

_____

_____

_____

_____

_____

_____

_____

_____

Day 2

Trust in the Lord with all your heart, and do not rely on your own insight. In all your ways acknowledge him, and he will make straight your paths.

Proverbs 3:5-6, NRSV

Susan was always a trusting person. She never met anyone she'd call a stranger. She was at a party one holiday weekend and left her drink unattended while she went to dance. That night changed the trajectory of her life. Someone had dropped a "roofie" in her drink. "Roofies" are the street name for Rohypnol, the "date rape" drug. She began to seize and eventually went into a coma which lasted for weeks. I was so afraid she would die. I fussed and complained for days to anyone who would listen about the consequences of trusting people. You see, I'm an untrusting skeptic. I live on the mantra that "I believe people just as far as I can throw them and my throwing arm is weak." But not Susan, she came out of that coma just as trusting as before. When asked how she felt about the event she replied, "I made the mistake of leaving my drink unattended. This was a lesson learned concerning responsibility not trust."

"I have to trust life. I can't live in fear. I trust God to protect me. Today, I'm alive to tell my story and help someone else be more responsible concerning their decisions and actions." That's Susan for you and I believe God sent her in my life to help me learn to let go of fear and learn to trust again.

Today I trust that -

_____

_____

_____

_____

_____

_____

_____

_____

_____

_____

_____

_____

_____

Day 3

Jesus said to him, "If you are able! All things can be done for the one who believes." Immediately the father of the child cried out "I believe; help my unbelief!"

Mark 9:23-24 NRSV

Today I was reading a devotional and the topic for the day was "fixated hope." Fixated hope is faith that has been constricted, controlled, and purposely dictated. It having faith that things are going to work out in certain areas in specific ways within certain time restraints.

My mind rehearsed the definition and explanation throughout the entire day. I started to remember what I learned about the word faith. My pastor said "faith is believing God in face of the facts." My seminary professor made the statement that, "faith is the thing that keeps you moving forward, right alongside of your fears.

That devotional reading helped me to realize that I had been lying to myself. I thought I was practicing a life of faith when in actuality, I was afraid to trust the God of my understanding to do the very things I was praying They* would do. Today I am learning to let go of outcomes and how I think God should do things. Today my prayer is, "Lord help my unbelief."

---

*They refers to a genderless God that encompasses male and female attributes.

Today I trust that -

_____

_____

_____

_____

_____

_____

_____

_____

_____

_____

_____

_____

_____

Day 4

The Lord will keep you from all evil; he will keep your life.

Psalms 121:7 NRSV

I was a victim of a robbery. My friends and I went to our high school's football game and these guys kept heckling and badgering us. After the game, they kept up this routine as they followed us to my car. When we got to the car, one guy pushed my friend Chris and he fell. I told the guys, "We didn't want any trouble." I suggested that we all go our separate ways? That's when I noticed one of the guys had walked up behind me. I wasn't sure what he was trying to do but before I could move away, he snatched my phone out of my hand and ran. The others looked at us to see what our response would be. We got into the car. As the guys walked off, I saw that one had a gun in his hand.

Thoughts of that night ran through my mind for weeks. I became very cautious about my surroundings and sometimes fearful to be out at night. But, I remember a prayer my mom would ask me to say every morning, "Lord save me, Lord protect me, Lord help me make good decisions." I didn't think about it much at first and I didn't feel like I was protected the night I was robbed. But when it's all said and done, I thank God for our lives. I believe God protected us that night. I believe God honored that prayer and sustained our lives. Today I am alive because I believe God hears and answers prayer.

Today I trust that -

_____

_____

_____

_____

_____

_____

_____

_____

_____

_____

_____

_____

Day 5

For the Lord has called you like a wife forsaken and grieved in spirit, like the wife of a man's youth when she is cast off, says your God.

Isaiah 54:6 NRSV

I am a female, ordained, Interdenominational minister living in the Bible-Belt. I've successfully worked with several local congregations but never once offered a salaried position. I served as an assistant pastor for three years without a stipend and now it's happening again. I'm attending a small church and I love it. However, I am not doing all I know to do or have been asked to do because of the hurt and resentment I carry from past experiences. Sometimes, I pray and ask God why I was called to ministry in an area that stifles and overlooks the call to ministry in women. There have been times when I've doubted God, doubted the call to ministry, and desired to throw in the towel.

But God is so awesome and patient. Every time these feelings overwhelm me and I began to pray, I'm drawn into a time of refreshing. It's during these times that my faith and hope are renewed in God and once again I believe God to do what God said would get done through me. I trust God to present the right opportunity before me at the right time. Until then, I rest in my belief in an all-powerful, all-knowing God.

Today I trust that -

_____

_____

_____

_____

_____

_____

_____

_____

_____

_____

_____

_____

Day 6

*As a deer longs for flowing streams, so my soul
longs for you, O God, My soul thirsts for God,
   for the living God.*

Psalm 42:1-2 NRSV

*Guard me as the apple of the eye; hide me in the
shadow of your wings…*

Psalm 17:8, NRSV

I was reading the Psalms for my morning
meditation and I began to consider a sermon I heard
years before. The preacher was teaching about
God's Holy Spirit when he gave this illustration.

A deer is being hunted by a wolf and is chased in
and out of the woods. If it is available, a deer will
seek out a body of water to run to. Why? Because
the water will cover his scent and quench his thirst.

This is a wonderful metaphor for God's Holy Spirit.
When I put my trust in God, God's Spirit covers me
and protects me from greater harm. When I pray
and believe that the God of my understanding hears
and honors that prayer, I am refreshed.

Today I trust that -

_____

_____

_____

_____

_____

_____

_____

_____

_____

_____

_____

_____

_____

Day 7

Then Peter began to speak to them: "I truly understand that God shows no partiality, but in every nation anyone who fears him and does what is right is acceptable to him.

Acts 10:34-35 NRSV

I love the Matrix movies. I cried like a baby when I saw the first episode of the trilogy. The Wakowskis had managed to make a movie out of the very things I thought about but dared to voice.

I was watching a documentary about the Wakowskis and learned that getting the movie makers to produce The Matrix wasn't an easy task. The Wakowskis went to Warner Brother Studios for financial backing but Warner wasn't interested.The Wakowskis didn't give up but went on to prove themselves by producing a low-budget film that brought them rave reviews. That convinced Warner to fund their project. The Matrix made 173 million dollars at the box office alone. Warner Brother executives were quoted saying, "We wish they (the Wakowskis) would never leave."

It took bold, steadfast belief in their creative genius for the dream of the Wakowskis to come true. It took consistent belief in their vision for The Matrix Trilogies to be realized. Today I believe in the gifts, talents and creative genius God has given me and I trust that my consistent work and forward movement will bring me similar results.

Today I trust that -

_____

_____

_____

_____

_____

_____

_____

_____

_____

_____

_____

_____

_____

_____

The Challenge to Change

Everything and everyone is in a constant state of change. It's inevitable. Oftentimes, challenges are approached reluctantly due to the perceived notion that they are, or involve, considerable work. The real challenge comes when we struggle with the inevitable.

Most everyone desires better; a better life, better health, a better job, and more. Desiring better is not always about power, competition, or greed. Sometimes our personal, internal measure of success drives us to work towards better. This is not to confuse gratitude for our present lives and accomplishments. This is a growing anxiety attached to the knowledge that there is always room for growth.

There are other times in our lives that we profess contentment only to find ourselves forced into a situation that demands change. The choice is ours. We must learn to accept the challenge (or challenges) to change or live a stagnant or paralyzed existence.

Change is inevitable. The next seven days you are invited to take on the challenges that life offers us to change. Whether we willingly or unwillingly accept the challenge or not, change is coming. Remember, everything and everyone changes. The challenge is to accept it and allow the transition to take you where you want to go.

Today I accept the challenge to -

_____

_____

_____

_____

_____

_____

_____

_____

_____

_____

_____

_____

_____

Day 1

Therefore, since we are surrounded by so great a cloud of witnesses, let us also lay aside every weight and the sin that clings so closely, and let us run with perseverance the race that is set before us…

Hebrews 12:1 NRSV

I had a dream about a hot air balloon. It was colorful and beautiful and ready to fly. However, it was weighted down by a group of sand bags. When I would look up at the hot air balloon, my heart would soar and I could imagine the wind on my face as I began to fly. But when I looked down at the sand bags, I grew angry and disgusted.

When I awoke the next morning the feelings I felt in my dream continued to resonate with me. The radio was playing in the background while I dressed and something called "Morning Motivation Moments" began to play. The speaker said these words with R. Kelly's *I Believe I Could Fly* playing in the background, "You were born to fly but the challenge is, will you give up the people, places, and things that are weighing you down?"

This was like an interpretation to my dream. The question echoed in my heart and my head, "will I give up what it takes to fly?" I'm not sure of who where, what, or when I'll have to give it all up but I'm willing to take the plunge and accept the challenge because more than anything, I am ready to fly.

Today I accept the challenge to -

_____

_____

_____

_____

_____

_____

_____

_____

_____

_____

_____

_____

_____

_____

Day 2

Do to others as you would have them do to you.

Luke 6:31 NRSV

I was reared by very compassionate and caring people. I remember how they would give to the church, schools, charities, and just homeless people on the street. When I was younger it would bother me. I didn't understand how they would give all our money away to "those" people and not give me everything I asked.

As I grew older, that misunderstanding grew into a deep-seated hatred for anyone I thought was needy. I became selfish, greedy adult. The challenge came when my mother died. Where were all the people she helped ? I'll tell you where. They were at the funeral home making sure her family wouldn't have to suffer any financial burden. They were at the funeral by the thousands paying their respect and celebrating her life. They were at the house, on the phone, in my email, making sure I knew the legacy she had left behind.

The challenge was for me to change my perspective on giving, caring, and showing compassion for humankind. The challenge was for me to accept that what I do while I live will determine the type of legacy I leave. My mother left a legacy of selfless love and concern. Now it was my turn to turn from greed and turn toward compassion. It may not be easy, but I will change.

Today I accept the challenge to -

_____

_____

_____

_____

_____

_____

_____

_____

_____

_____

_____

Day 3

"Other seed fell into good soil and brought forth grain, growing up and increasing and yielding thirty and sixty and a hundredfold."

Mark 4:8 NRSV

We were Bible toting, tithe paying members. When we started our business we felt obligated to pay at least 10% to the church. There were times when we were so grateful that we'd pay 15% or 20% of our income back to the church or some local charity.

Our income was effected drastically after the housing market fell and we were forced to scale back our style of life. There was no way we could continue to tithe but we tried to give a small offering when it was convenient.

I was cooking dinner one night and listening to Mark Chirrona. He was teaching from Mark chapter four about the thirty, sixty, one hundred fold. Suddenly I felt ashamed. How could our faith fail us in this season? If we believed God during times of plenty, the challenge was to believe God in this time of scarcity. The challenge is not to decrease our giving but to increase it. We started budgeting 5% to give to the church. It eventually grew back to 10% and sometimes 15%. We accepted the challenge to give regardless of our financial situation and our lives changed forever. Today business is thriving and we believe it's the result of accepting the challenge to change how we think about giving.

Today I accept the challenge to -

_____

_____

_____

_____

_____

_____

_____

_____

_____

_____

_____

_____

_____

Day 4

I am confident of this, that the one
who began a good work among you will bring it to
completion by the day of Jesus Christ.

Philippians 1:6 NRSV

Earlean started her non-profit organization over ten years ago. It's been a difficult journey. Funding was always a problem but she managed to stay encouraged. Besides, things had slowly gotten better over the years.

Earlean had a clear vision for the future of her organization and funding was a critical part of that vision. However, writing and receiving grants became an increasingly competitive arena. There were more organizations and agencies going after the same funds. She thought about cutting their losses and closing down. But, the passion for her vision kept her moving forward.

An old song came on the radio while she was driving to a meeting with some perspective funders. It was from a Sheri Jones- Moffet CD. There was a preaching monologue at the beginning of the song and it said, "God started it and He'll finish it, but you've got to work the middle." Wow! Just like that, Earlean knew she couldn't give up. Those words made her more determined to accept this challenge of the in-between time. "Working the middle" was the key ingredient to changing her outlook and seeing the vision unfold. Earlean worked her middle and got the funding.

Today I accept the challenge to -

_____

_____

_____

_____

_____

_____

_____

_____

_____

_____

_____

Day 5

Elijah then came near to all the people, and said,
"How long will you go limping with two different
opinions? If the Lord is God, follow him; but if
Baal, then follow him." The people did not answer
him a word.

1Kings 18:21 NRSV

My aunt Jennie had a way with words. She would
use the simplest of clichés to offer solutions to an
array of problems. I didn't pay attention or take into
consideration the things she would say when I was
younger but time and challenges will bring on
change.

I always considered myself a thorough person;
weighing all the variables before making a final
decision. It was the voice of reason and an old
cliché that helped me to realize that what I was
actually doing was called procrastination. I went
back and forth in my mind and on paper for five
years concerning opening a business. Finally, one
night during prayer I heard my Aunt Jennies voice.
She said, "Piss or get off the pot."

The simplicity of these words offered a challenge to
change. Doing one or the other demands that a
decision be made. This was a wake-up call. I had sat
on my "pot" for too long. If I was ever going to
make a change and move out, I needed to take a piss
or simply get up.

Today I accept the challenge to -

_____

_____

_____

_____

_____

_____

_____

_____

_____

_____

_____

_____

_____

_____

Day 6

Take my yoke upon you, and learn from me; for I am gentle and humble in heart, and you will find rest for your souls. For my yoke is easy, and my burden is light."

Matthew 11:29-30 NRSV

Have you ever read something and gained Biblical knowledge? That's what happened to me one morning. While reading an article about animals yoked together for the purposes of farming, the word yoke reminded me of a scripture; Matthew 11:29-30. When I read it. I was reminded that we have a choice to take on the yoke of Jesus.

If we are true to ourselves, we would have to admit that we are probably "yoked" with people that are causing us resistance. Sometimes that can be hard to admit but maybe that's the case. Maybe we are tied to the wrong people and they are the reason we are experiencing pressure and problems in our lives.

What if you were going straight towards your goal in life and the person you're "yoked-up" with decides they want to bear to the left? Then the one that holds the reigns has to use greater force to keep you both on track. This challenged me to examine those I have been connected to. I wanted to ensure that if I'm experiencing pressure or delays because of someone else, that a change has to be made.

The yoke of Jesus should be easy. The challenge is to take up that yoke and keep your eyes on the prize.

Today I accept the challenge to -

_____

_____

_____

_____

_____

_____

_____

_____

_____

_____

_____

_____

_____

Day 7

"But you, take courage! Do not let your hands be weak, for your work shall be rewarded."

2 Chron.15:7 NRSV

There's some confusion to who said it but the saying goes, *"The definition of insanity is doing the same thing over and over and expecting it to come out different."*

As a recovering co-dependent I know how relentless the fight can be with insane thoughts. Thoughts which lead you to believe that if you give your all to others than they will eventually and diligently reciprocate. I know, it sounds like pure insanity, but it's something that we find ourselves habitually doing.

I've spent so much time, effort, and money in helping others that it actually inconvenienced me and my family. Then after I was broke, busted, and disgusted, no-one was around to help us.

But the insanity stopped when I made the determination that it was time to change. It took courage to stop and courage to change my old routine. It was uncomfortable at first because it was challenging my old belief system. But, eventually I experienced a fresh difference. This happened because I dared to stop the insanity, therefore making a change in my life.

Today I accept the challenge to -

_____

_____

_____

_____

_____

_____

_____

_____

_____

_____

_____

_____

_____

Differentiate: Enemy or Inner-Me

There are times in our lives when we feel like bulls in a china store. Every decision is a poor one. Every move is the wrong one. We feel as if we are losing control of our lives. Suddenly we are so stressed out that the idea of taking responsibility for so many screw-ups is unimaginable. We find ourselves saying, like Flip Wilson's character Geraldine , "The devil made me do it."

As a practicing Christian, I learned early that there is an enemy out there in the world waiting to sabotage the lives of the saints. The more I prayed and studied the more I felt that there had to be something more than "the devil" hindering my efforts. I had to learn to differentiate.

I believe there are evil forces out in the world, just like there are good ones. However, I believe that if we are true to ourselves, we'd find that the central source of most of our problems and failures comes from within. Myles Monroe was the first person I ever heard describe this dilemma as the inner-me.

As we move through our various processes and are presented with road blocks along the way; we must differentiate between what is really blocking us and determine if it is the enemy or our inner-me. Performing this task is an act of responsibility and accountability that will help advance us forward.

Don't be afraid to take responsibility for those poor decisions of the past. Don't be afraid to admit it was your inner-me that stirred you wrong. Don't be afraid to be true to yourself. Differentiate!

Today, I take responsibility for-

_____

_____

_____

_____

_____

_____

_____

_____

_____

_____

_____

_____

_____

_____

Day 1

Do not be conformed to this world but be transformed by the renewing of your minds, so that you may discern what is the will of God—what is good and acceptable and perfect.

Romans 12:2 NRSV

I was married to a drug addict for over nine years. We tried everything to get him healthy. I tried prayer, bargaining with God, and being the ideal wife while he went in and out of treatment centers. Finally, I had enough. I made the decision and an appointment to visit the last treatment center he entered before our divorce. I didn't go to visit him but to speak with his psychiatrist to put our heads together and come up with a plan to finally get my husband sober. It was now or never. If this didn't work, divorce was inevitable.

The doctor was very interested in what I had to say, careful not to strategize a plan for my husband's disease but instead provided a plan for my own healing. I didn't know it at the time, but when that doctor sent me to A-Anon, it changed my life. I learned I was a co-addicted, co-dependent, an enabler. My thoughts were making me emotionally sick. I learned the difference between genuine love and the warped emotion I thought was love for so long. It was a process that taught me to replace old beliefs about myself with new affirming ones. I learned to differentiate between loving someone else and trying to control them. Today, we're divorced, but now I know how to love because I learned to love me.

Today, I take responsibility for-

_____

_____

_____

_____

_____

_____

_____

_____

_____

_____

_____

_____

_____

_____

Day 2

Love is patient; love is kind; love is not envious or boastful or arrogant

I Corinthians 13:4 NRSV

Nine years living with an active drug abuser gives you an easy-out when things aren't going as well as you'd like. For instance, if I'm tired, broke, or late, I could blame on it on them. It was a fail proof strategy. No one ever challenged my story, and I always received plenty of empathy. Some people even saw me as a courageous saint with the patience of Job.

That worked for me for a long time - nine years to be exact. Eventually, life felt like an ongoing theatrical performance. The truth is I was always tired due to the stress of living with an addict. I was broke most of the time because I gave him access to my account and I was always late because I rarely knew where my car was after lending it to him.

For nine years, the theatrical side of my existence and reality were blurred. I had a difficult time differentiating between the things I knew to do and the things I actually did. For years, my "inner-me" felt I had to meet his needs at the cost of my own. Today, I take responsibility for my own happiness and welfare. We aren't together any longer, but that's the results of me taking care of me.

Today I take responsibility for-

_____

_____

_____

_____

_____

_____

_____

_____

_____

_____

_____

_____

_____

_____

_____

Day 3

You ask and do not receive, because you ask wrongly, in order to spend what you get on your pleasures.

James 4:3 NRSV

A young lady at the church spoke with me concerning her marriage. Her husband was verbally, emotionally, and physically abusive. She asked why God was not responding to her prayers to make her husband the man she felt he was called to be. She envisioned him as a leader in the church, a loving man that cherished her, and made her feel loved. Why wasn't her prayer being answered? Why was he still abusive?

I touched her gently on her hand and shared, "God loves us all and gives us all free will. There may be a difference between what your husband wants and what you want for him. There is something you can do to help your situation. Make a differentiation between those things that you can control in order to protect yourself."

She looked bewildered but agreed, and we ended our talk with prayer. This time we prayed to God for wisdom, clarity, and the power to know the difference between what those things she can do for herself and those things that are beyond her control. We also prayed that she comes to understand God's desires for her life and the power of acceptance if that does not include her husband.

Today, I take responsibility for-

_____

_____

_____

_____

_____

_____

_____

_____

_____

_____

_____

_____

_____

Day 4

*Let each of you look not only to his own interests,
but also to the interests of others.*

Philippians 2:4 NRSV

I have a friend that started smoking when she was
twelve years old. She said peer-pressure made her
do it. A cup of coffee and a cigarette or a glass of
wine and cigarette were said to make you look cool.
It also became the stylish thing to do in college
instead of eating. My friend explained it like
someone was holding her at gunpoint and making
her light each cigarette and take every drink.

Today, she still smokes but now her excuse is "if I
stop I'll gain weight. Besides I'm a busy woman
that needs a cigarette from time to time to relax." In
addition to all that, she makes no qualms about
smoking because, as she says, "I can stop when I
get ready, but I don't really smoke that much."

I'm afraid my friend is shortening her life because
she's unable or unwilling to differentiate between
what's important. She has been unable or unwilling
to take responsibility for her actions and therefore
for her life. I'm afraid that her not being able or
willing to accept this as truth is going to kill her. I
love her enough to point these things out, but I love
myself enough to not love her more than she loves
herself. She has to take responsibility and
differentiate between what looks and feels good and
what's actually good.

Today, I take responsibility for-

_____

_____

_____

_____

_____

_____

_____

_____

_____

_____

_____

_____

_____

Day 5

You are the God who works wonders; you have displayed your might among the peoples.

Psalm 77:14 NRSV

Money was extremely tight after my husband left us. I lost plenty of sleep pondering and praying over whether we should try to keep our house or rent an apartment. I didn't know if we could pay our house note, but I didn't have the money to move either.

One day I decided to be brave and talk with the lender. They gave me the numbers to several resources known for helping individuals in this position, but I kept praying. I needed a miracle from God. Six stressful months later, I decided to call one of those resources. In many ways, I felt like my faith was wavering and I was giving up on myself and God.

Conditions arose about halfway through the process. I was about to throw in the towel when a light bulb came on and brought clarity to my weary mind. Who am I to say who God will or will not use? Who am I to say that a resource isn't a miracle? At that moment, I made the differentiation between waiting on God as an excuse and waiting on God for clarity. Today, I accept responsibility for my life. I do those things I can and allow God to do the things I can't. Meanwhile, I take advantage of God's favor through the many resources in the earth today. Today, eight years later, my son and I still own our home.

Today, I take responsibility for-

_____

_____

_____

_____

_____

_____

_____

_____

_____

_____

_____

_____

_____

_____

Day 6

But Martha was distracted by her many tasks; so she came to him and asked, "Lord, do you not care that my sister has left me to do all the work by myself? Tell her then to help me." But the Lord answered her, "Martha, Martha, you are worried and distracted by many things; there is need of only one thing Mary has chosen the better part, which will not be taken away from her."

Luke 10:40-42 NRSV

The New Year brought loads of opportunities. I accepted a full-time position as a counselor, one of the local pastors signed a contract to use my non-profit for its counseling services, and I am negotiating a deal with another pastor for the same. It felt like my prayers were being answered.

Being stuck in the house on a snow day gave me time to reflect and thank God for every opportunity. It is my prayer that I exhaust all there is out of every opportunity presented to me. However, during reflection, I realized that every opportunity maybe a good opportunity but not necessarily a God opportunity. It was time for me to make that distinction. I was certainly busy, but was I productive?

Each opportunity brought a sense of fulfillment, but it robbed me of family time and my time with God. My child's grades were slipping and my peace of mind too. It was time for me to take responsibility for my decisions and differentiate between what feels good and what is good for me and my family.

Today, I take responsibility for-

_____

_____

_____

_____

_____

_____

_____

_____

_____

_____

_____

_____

_____

_____

Day 7

My sheep hear my voice. I know them, and they follow me.

John 10:27 NRSV

One day, I was walking my dogs and enjoying the view. I like to think of our morning walks as my morning meditation. I use this time to pray and reflect over a myriad of topics.

One day, it occurred to me that if I lived anywhere else in the world, my view of God might be different. The things I hear and attribute to God's voice maybe considered the voice of reason or my subconscious speaking. That's when I realized that the voice we hear in our head, our mind, or our spirit is shaped by our individual contexts. If I were reared in a country or environment that believed God only spoke through a priest or that there was no such thing as God, then I would probably think the voice I hear is imagined or my mind recovering memories of things said in the past.

This revelation didn't shake my faith. I still believe God speaks to and through me. However, it has caused me to stop and make a determination between what I heard and who I heard. I have to admit. I've used "God said it" as an excuse more than once when attempting to avoid responsibility for my decisions. Truth is, whether we believe God said a thing or not, we have been given the awesome responsibility of earthly dominion and with that comes free-will. Refuse to use "God said it" as an excuse. Use free-will wisely.

Today, I take responsibility for-

_____

_____

_____

_____

_____

_____

_____

_____

_____

_____

_____

_____

_____

_____

Evaluate

I was driving home from work one night and began to pray. As the prayer went forth with praise and acknowledgement of the God of my understanding, my mind went back to an earlier time in my life. There was a time that I questioned everything I was ever taught about God. It was not that I didn't believe there was a Power greater than humankind but because I desired to personally know this Power.

So I began to evaluate everything I was ever taught about God. I was warned by fellow Christians not to question God. Although the Bible they so often "misquote" declares that if we want wisdom, we should ask God (James 1:5). Others told me not to expose myself to the evils of different beliefs, but If God is greater than, why should we fear other beliefs? If God was (and is) God, then I wanted to know that God for myself.

Today, I attribute the awesome relationship I have with God to that time of searching and evaluation. Today, I believe in the God that is not offended by our search to know more about Them*. Today, I see the quest to know and the desire to search and evaluate the God of your family's understanding as a gift from the only wise God. We become educated, enlightened, and empowered if we accept this gift of evaluation. Don't be afraid to know the God you serve. Evaluate your present knowledge and relationship of God and come closer to deliverance.

*Them is used to recognize the Triune Godhead.

Today's evaluation revealed

_____

_____

_____

_____

_____

_____

_____

_____

_____

_____

_____

_____

_____

_____

Day 1

Before the mountains were brought forth,
or ever you had formed the earth and the world,
from everlasting to everlasting you are God.

Psalm 90:2 NRSV

One day, I began to day dream about how my life would have turned out had I been born, reared, or even lived in another country. Questions began to arise. Questions like: "Would I still believe in God?" "Would I still believe Jesus is the Son of God?" "Would I be a Christian?" The more I thought about it, the more I realized the likelihood that I would have a very different belief system.

This made me evaluate what I presently believe about God. Things like: God is love, God is the creator of all, and God is omniscient, omnipresent, and omnipotent. These are some of the foundational beliefs I have concerning the God of my understanding. If I truly believe these things about God, then I don't think it really matters where I live or what faith I profess. God has got to be greater.

As I continued to evaluate the matter, I realized that God crosses all gender, racial, ethnic, denominational, socio-economic, educational, and sexual orientation lines. This is great because the world needs a God that is more powerful than its problems. A God this big and powerful is not offended by who we are or where we are. This God is from everlasting to everlasting.

Today's evaluation revealed

_____

_____

_____

_____

_____

_____

_____

_____

_____

_____

_____

_____

_____

_____

Day 2

*Take delight in the L*ORD*, and he will give you the*
desires of your heart. Commit your way to
*the L*ORD*; trust in him, and he will act.*
                                        Psalm 37:4-5 NRSV

Fifteen years ago, I accepted the task of starting a
non-profit organization that would be a ministry
tool and resource for the church as well as the
business sector. We were a "grass-roots'
organization. Opportunities to display our benefits
and raise funds were hard to come by, but we
continued to plan and pray.

This year our prayers have seemed to be answered
all at once. Opportunities began to flow in our
direction: an opportunity to work full time that
would eventually give us what we needed in terms
of finances, knowledge and resources, a weekly
opportunity that would provide us with less money
but greater prospects among the Christian
community, another opportunity that would provide
greater flexibility along with additional finances,
and lastly, an ongoing, smaller opportunity that
would allow me to use my creativity and make
some personal money. All of these opportunities
appeared to be answers to our prayers. We had to
evaluate the pros and cons of each and determine
which was right for us in this season. That
evaluation led us to understand that not only will
God give us the desires of our heart through
answered prayers, but God will give us what things
to desire.

Today's evaluation revealed

_____

_____

_____

_____

_____

_____

_____

_____

_____

_____

_____

_____

_____

Day 3

Death and life are in the power of the
tongue, and those who love it will eat its fruits.

Proverbs 18:21 NRSV

No one would probably ever believe it, but I was a shy, introverted child. I prayed to be assertive and outspoken like some of my peers. I'm not sure when, but my prayers were answered, and I came to be known for my quick wit and painful honesty. I learned to take pride in this acquired aspect of my personality... Until I started seminary.

It was in seminary that I learned the power of silence. Silence is a discipline that displays peace and power. I was taught that there is a "Ministry of Presence," where we learn to serve others by just being there. I learned through the reading of the biblical text that silence is a wartime strategy that could easily diffuse or confuse the enemy.

I also learned the power of the spoken word. Carefully chosen words can build us while carelessly chosen words can destroy us. The true mastery of all this knowledge is hidden within our ability to evaluate situations and circumstances while simultaneously disciplining our tongues. Some situations will call for the "Ministry of Presence" and the peace that dwells therein. Other situations will require carefully chosen spoken words. Our task is to appropriately evaluate the time and circumstance for each.

Today's evaluation revealed

_____

_____

_____

_____

_____

_____

_____

_____

_____

_____

_____

_____

_____

_____

Day 4

But grow in the grace and knowledge of our Lord and Savior Jesus Christ. To him be the glory both now and to the day of eternity. Amen.

2Peter 3:18 NRSV

Like most growing boys, our son Dru went through several obsessions. While in middle school, he became enamored with Pokémon. He studied everything about them. His goal was to amass an army of evolved Pokémon for battle with other enthusiasts.

One day he was riding with me to run some errands when he became increasingly frustrated with one particular Pokémon. It appeared that Pokémon evolved into their more powerful alter egos after a certain number of battles with other Pokémon and that didn't seem to be the case that day. After hours of battling, Dru turned to me and said, "That's it…I'm trading this Pokémon because it's a waste of time…he won't evolve."

His words brought on immediate self-evaluation. God used Dru to show me how I allowed my frustrations to keep me from evolving. I was so busy fighting to make things happen that I failed to trust God in the process. Today, I practice self-evolution as a tool to insure that I am always growing in grace and in the knowledge of our Lord and savior Jesus Christ. I would hate to be traded.

Today's evaluation revealed

Day 5

Trust in the LORD, and do good; so you will live in the land, and enjoy security.

Psalm 37:3 NRSV

Our son has loved being in the water all of his life. His father and I started him with swim lessons as an infant. Still, he developed a fear of putting his head under water as he became older. We didn't push him to get over this fear but just kept taking him to the pool and the beach. He loved playing in the water.

One day, we were enjoying a warm day at the pool when I noticed Dru standing at the edge of the deep end of the pool. I carefully watched him as he accessed the area. He stood there looking for what felt like an hour. Then, without notice, he jumped in the pool. I started toward him but waited for him to trust his instincts and before long he came to the top with the biggest grin on his face. He couldn't wait to get out of the pool and do it over and over again.

We could all gain insight from what Dru did that day. Learn to take the time and evaluate what stands before you and then jump right in and trust that you will rise to the top.

Today's evaluation revealed

_____

_____

_____

_____

_____

_____

_____

_____

_____

_____

_____

_____

_____

_____

Day 6

Be careful then how you live, not as unwise people but as wise, making the most of the time, because the days are evil. So do not be foolish, but understand what the will of the Lord is.

Ephesians 5:15-17 NRSV

Years ago when a dear friend of my mine died, I decided to keep in touch with her aging mother. Twice a month, I would pick her up and bring her to my house to do her hair, have lunch, and run errands. It was an event we both looked forward to.

As the years went by and my schedule grew busier, I found myself making excuses for not keeping our monthly appointments. The more I tried to justify why I couldn't keep our monthly schedule, the heavier I felt. Finally, I woke up early one morning and couldn't go back to sleep. I got dressed to go for a walk and to pray. I heard the word "prioritize" and immediately began to set my day in order. Just as I was about to feel proud of my arranged schedule, I heard the word again, "prioritize." Suddenly, a light came on and I rearranged my day to include my dear friend's mom.

It was on that day that I learned that no matter how we access and evaluate matters, our evaluation must always begin with God. Not only does what we do for Christ last, it can redeem time.

Today's evaluation revealed

_____

_____

_____

_____

_____

_____

_____

_____

_____

_____

_____

_____

_____

_____

Day 7

Test me, Lord, and try me, examine my heart and my mind;

Psalm 26:2 NRSV

I spent a couple of years working at a women's substance abuse treatment center. There was a cycle that most of the clients would go through during the onset, the middle, and the final phases of treatment. During the onset of treatment, every lady would exhibit some combination of anxiety in the form of fear and apprehension. During the middle stages of treatment, the ladies would display a multitude of personas as they started to learn who they were. Lastly, during the final phases of treatment they would let down their guards and open their hearts and minds to fully embrace what treatment could do for them.

The funny thing about this cycle is it's during the early phases of treatment that clients would often express their readiness for change. It's only during the final phases of their treatment that they begin to realize that weren't as ready as they believed. My job as their counselor is to evaluate their responses and behaviors to help determine when they truly are ready for change and to successfully complete our program. Past evaluations have proved that it's only when we become vulnerable and accept the process of change that we will discipline ourselves to live healthy, balanced lives.

Today's evaluation revealed

_____

_____

_____

_____

_____

_____

_____

_____

_____

_____

_____

_____

_____

_____

Forgive

Forgiveness is a foreign concept. It is not foreign to us as it relates to familiarity with the term, but foreign as it relates to our genuine understanding of the mechanics of forgiveness. How does the victim extending forgiveness to the perpetrator help them? How does harboring un-forgiveness harm us?

Forgiveness is a form of release from the confines and controls of its counterpart, un-forgiveness. When we forgive those who have perpetrated great evils against us, we release our minds from obsessively thinking about the situation. We release our hearts to learn to love and trust again. We release our bodies from the by-products of stress to a state of healing and balance.

Forgiveness is a system of release. Trying to understand it will rob it of its mystery. Forgiveness has to be embraced so that the power of it can resonate in the hearts of those that do so and implode. Implosion is accompanied by a greater capacity to live, laugh, and love.

Forgiveness is a tool from God that surpasses human understanding. It's a selfish act that reaps unselfish rewards. With all that forgiveness does for the victim, it is equally healing for the perpetrator. Who can go unchanged when they know they have been forgiven? Consider that fact for the next week and move closer toward freedom and deliverance.

Today, I forgive

_____

_____

_____

_____

_____

_____

_____

_____

_____

_____

_____

_____

_____

_____

Day 1

For if you forgive others their trespasses, your heavenly Father will also forgive you;

Matthew 6:14, NRSV

I was full of ideas and zeal when first entering ministry. I had the opportunity to help several pastors' plant new churches throughout the city. There was one pastor that had been struggling with how to be more involved with the community surrounding his church site. I shared a wonderful idea that I knew would serve our congregation, the neighborhood high school, and the students well. He was excited and called for a meeting of the church's leaders to make the proposal. The day of the meeting, that pastor pitched my idea to the church's leaders as if God had revealed it directly to him. I tried to appease my anger with thoughts like, "All that's important is that the work gets done," but resentment continued to rise.

The level of anger and disappointment that brewed within left me feeling foolish and used. That seed of bitterness caused me to distrust pastors while souring my passion for ministry. It took lots of prayer and reflection before realizing that those who were suffering weren't the perpetrators. I had to forgive that pastor in order to refuel my passion for ministry. It wasn't easy because pride wanted me to stay bitter, but I did and I am free to serve today.

Today, I forgive

_____

_____

_____

_____

_____

_____

_____

_____

_____

_____

_____

_____

_____

Day 2

Put away from you all bitterness and wrath and anger and wrangling and slander, together with all malice, and be kind to one another, tenderhearted, forgiving one another, as God in Christ has forgiven you.

Ephesians 4:31-32 NRSV

Early one morning, my son and I had an intense argument concerning his lackadaisical attitude. He missed the bus to school, and in order for both of us to get to our destinations on time, we would have to move quickly. He didn't seem concerned. I lost it. It appeared to me that I was being disrespected and I raised my voice to tell him so. He lost it and accused me of hollering and screaming for no reason. I didn't understand his accusation. I couldn't follow his train of thought, so I stood there and just looked at him.

That event troubled me greatly. Later that evening, he texted me an apology. I couldn't respond. It was like the culmination of hurt from everyone I ever loved and cared for crashed in on me. I wasn't just angry at my son. I was angry at everyone that I loved and thought loved me.

I felt betrayed by the people I loved. Some lied, others cheated, but they all eventually left. I couldn't accept my son's apology because I was harboring un-forgiveness towards many. It hasn't happened yet, but I'm working daily to forgive each and every one of them. My life and sanity depends upon it.

Today, I forgive

_____

_____

_____

_____

_____

_____

_____

_____

_____

_____

_____

_____

_____

_____

Day 3

Pride goes before destruction, and a haughty spirit before a fall.

Proverbs 16:18 NRSV

I pride myself on a lot of things. One of which is not accepting everything offered like an apology. I have a routine when it comes to apologies. I will acknowledge it, thank you for it, but not quickly accept it.

I never thought much about why I have this theory until I started writing forgiveness stories for this devotional. Today, I can attribute my actions to plain ole' vengeance and pride. When someone hurts me, I want them to hurt as much or more and when they apologize, I want them to believe that I am so important that they should work for my acceptance. It's not that this routine has any positive purpose. In retrospect, it has only provided negative side effects.

Forgiveness can provide healing for the victim and the perpetrator when apologies are offered. Our selfish desire to withhold forgiveness is an attempt to make our perpetrators suffer. This very act can cause us to suffer longer as well as run the risk of un-forgiveness turning into unresolved resentment. Don't allow pride and ignorance to keep you from the restorative powers of forgiveness today.

Today, I forgive

_____

_____

_____

_____

_____

_____

_____

_____

_____

_____

_____

_____

_____

_____

Day 4

Bear with one another and, if anyone has a complaint against another, forgive each other; just as the Lord has forgiven you, so you also must forgive.

Colossians 3:13 NRSV

Years ago, I was an assistant manager of a chain hair salon. I was in charge of the practical portion of the hiring process. One day one of my church members came to apply for a stylist position and it was my task to determine if her work was polished enough to hire her. It wasn't. She had very elementary skills, but I decided I wanted to help a fellow church member. I offered her a deal. I would tell the manager she passed if she would agree to stay after hours for training. She agreed and eventually became one of highest producing stylists.

After several years passed, her confidence evolved into jealousy. I began to hear little rumors about how she felt I was a weak manager and even weaker stylist. I tried to speak with her on several occasions, but she would brush me off and accuse me of being paranoid.

Years later, after opening my own salon, I received a letter of apology from that stylist. I didn't accept her apology. I kept that letter as proof of how wrong she was and how righteous I thought I was. The need to be right caused me to harbor un-forgiveness. I finally learned that not forgiving her was forcing me to live in the past and denying me the chance to move forward. I chose to forgive.

Today, I forgive

_____

_____

_____

_____

_____

_____

_____

_____

_____

_____

_____

_____

_____

Day 5

*If you forgive the sins of any, they are forgiven
them; if you retain the sins of any, they are retained.*

John 20:23, NRSV

I loved and trusted my husband with all my heart. It
grieved me to learn he was having an affair. The
pain of that knowledge felt like someone had died.
It made me feel ugly, betrayed, and foolish.

I cried myself to sleep that night. The next morning,
I went to let our dog out and the blinds on the back
door were torn down. There was a trail of loose
stool across the entryway. Our pet had tried and
failed to wake me up or get the door opened, so he
could avoid using the bathroom in the house.

I quickly let him outside, cleaned up the mess,
replaced the blinds, and showed him I understood
and still loved him. Immediately, I thought about
how willing I was to forgive our dog but not my
husband. They both made mistakes and they both
deserved forgiveness.

Believe me, it took a lot longer for me to forgive my
husband than it did to forgive our pet, but he
apologized and eventually I did. Every time the
inclination to second guess and distrust him has
arisen, I remember the revelation of that day and
ask God to help me hold on to that forgiveness. It is
what has allowed us to live free and happy lives
from that day forward.

Today, I forgive

Day 6

Therefore, I tell you, her sins, which were many, have been forgiven; hence she has shown great love. But the one to whom little is forgiven, loves little."

Luke 7:47, NRSV

I was invited to attend a meeting of Christian women called Agape. A former Catholic but recently ordained protestant preacher from Switzerland was the guest speaker. His story was a love story about how he met and fell in love with his non Catholic wife. He explained being torn between obeying his heart and obeying his family and priest. He was attending a wedding when the priest said, "What God has put together, let no man put asunder…" A light came on and he realized God was answering his prayer. He concluded that if God is love and the giver of all things good, God had sent him his wife and it wasn't a surprise to God that she wasn't Catholic.

He ended his speech by telling us how it became important for him to forgive his parents, the Catholic Church, and the priest although they never actually asked for forgiveness by apologizing. He went on to share his understanding of love as the result of the revelation that was given him that day. If God is love, then we must love and forgiveness is a by-product of that love.

Today, I forgive

_____

_____

_____

_____

_____

_____

_____

_____

_____

_____

_____

_____

_____

_____

Day 7

*So now instead you should forgive and console him,
so that he may not be overwhelmed by excessive
sorrow.*

2 Corinthians 2:7, NRSV

I started a small support group for women who
have survived various forms of abuse. We were
doing a guided mediation when I had a moment of
clarification.

During the meditation, I saw my twelve-year-old
self. I was twelve years old when my father
molested me. The voice on the tape asked us to see
our present selves walk over to our younger selves
and allow the words to flow. The first thing out of
my mouth was, "Why didn't you fight back?" At
the end of the mediation, I felt an immense amount
of anger. For over forty years, I had been harboring
this resentment against myself for not fighting my
father off.

After the ladies left, I did some additional
meditation of my own. I got on my knees and laid
across my bed and began to envision my twelve-
year-old self. This time, I went to her and she said,
"It's time for you to forgive you. You were afraid.
You did the best you could do." I stayed in that
vision until I felt forgiveness in my physical body.
When I did, I got up from that floor lighter than I
ever remember feeling. It was that night that I
learned that sometimes we have to go back and give
ourselves a break by forgiving ourselves.

Today, I forgive

_____

_____

_____

_____

_____

_____

_____

_____

_____

_____

_____

_____

_____

_____

Grow

The word grow can be intriguing. The synonyms provide a glimpse into what's actually involved when we say we want to grow. Synonyms like "develop" and "mature" indicate progress through a poignant process.

Take for an example germination. Germination is the process through which a seed grows into a plant. It's a process that many of us minimize or overlook, but it's also a process that is full of revelation. A seed has to shed its present state through a course of events that involve break-through. Breaking through is never an easy task as it requires an explosion, and explosions only happen as the direct result of pressure. This is the secret to growth.

There are ideas, innovations, and miracles trapped inside each of us, waiting for an atmosphere conducive for growth. To grow means to embrace change. To change means to embrace being uncomfortable. Change is constant, but the decision to grow into what you were designed to be or to shrink, decline, and fail are personal decisions. No one can grow or make a change for you. To do so would cause dysfunction and eventually yield faulty results.

Allow this next week to strengthen and encourage you to accept the challenges and beauty of growth as you grasp the principles of deliverance. Growth can be challenging but that's why it's called "growing pains."

Today, I see growth

_____

_____

_____

_____

_____

_____

_____

_____

_____

_____

_____

_____

_____

_____

Day 1

Trust in the LORD with all your heart, and do not rely on your own insight.

Proverbs 3:5 NRSV

After a visit to the pediatrician for an annual exam, we were called in for a consultation with the doctor to review my son's lab results. The doctor was concerned that his vitamin D level was low. She shared her experience with other athletic teens. It appears that to increase muscle mass while your bones are still stretching and growing could easily stunt the growth process. She gave us a prescription, which we immediately filled, and our son started taking that afternoon.

A couple of days later, I was in the kitchen preparing breakfast when our son walked up behind me to ask a question. When I turned around, I noticed that I had to elevate my gaze to look directly at him. This was amazing. It appeared that he had grown overnight, but how could that be?

The fact of the matter is that it took longer than overnight. Time can be elusive when you trust the process and practice discipline. The facts are he took the vitamin D daily and over time he grew. The same can happen for us in every area of our lives if we trust the process and become discipline in our practices. One day, we'll look around and we would have grown too.

Today, I see growth

_____

_____

_____

_____

_____

_____

_____

_____

_____

_____

_____

_____

_____

Day 2

Then the LORD answered me and said: Write the vision; make it plain on tablets, so that a runner may read it. For there is still a vision for the appointed time, it speaks of the end, and does not lie. If it seems to tarry, wait for it; it will surely come, it will not delay.

Habakkuk 2:2-3 NRSV

It was a hot summer weekend in August and I had to leave my husband and son home alone. My husband made plans for he and our son to visit the home of one of his clients to see a new litter of Labrador puppies. Somehow I knew we would have a new addition to our family when I arrived back home.

There he was. This cute bundle of white fluff whom they named Spot. The first thing I noticed about Spot was the size of his feet. My husband and son were adamant that Spot would grow to be a middle sized dog, but I begged to differ. Spot's big feet were a direct indication of his impending size. Today, Spot is 12 years old, 70 pounds, and when he on his hind feet, he stands 5ft. 6 inches tall. Spot is far from being a middle sized dog.

Some of us have what might be considered "big feet." Our "big feet" are the ideas and dreams that are still to be realized in our lives. The task is to stay focused, set goals, and prepare ourselves. Then at the appointed time and place, the opportunity will arise that will allow us to grow into our "big feet."

Today, I see growth

Day 3

*I am the true vine, and my Father is the vinegrower.
He removes every branch in me that bears no fruit.
Every branch that bears fruit he prunes to make it
bear more fruit.*

John 15:1-2 NRSV

Outside the window of the den of my first home
was a Crepe Myrtle tree. It always appeared to be a
nuisance with all of the Bumble Bees it seemed to
attract and the falling flowers. I decided one day to
prune it back to the point that it wouldn't grow until
the following spring. I cut what used to be a tree
that stood over the roof of my house, down to no
more than a bush. Later that same summer, that tree
was wider and fuller than before.

Now that I am a seasoned homeowner and pretty
good yard keeper, I've learned that there is a certain
time of year to prune Crepe Myrtle trees if you want
them to increase their blooms and a certain way to
prune them to direct their growth.

What I learned by mistake has served as
encouragement over the years. There are seasons in
our lives that excess will need to be cut off if we are
to grow bigger and go further. Sure we may look
and feel awkward while in transition, but the end
result will yield abundance and growth.

Today, I see growth

_____

_____

_____

_____

_____

_____

_____

_____

_____

_____

_____

_____

_____

Day 4

Do not be conformed to this world, but be transformed by the renewing of your minds, so that you may discern what is the will of God what is good and acceptable and perfect.

Romans 12:2 NRSV

I read a story online some years ago about a pond near a chemical waste plant. This pond was full of tadpoles that eventually grew into frogs. However, these frogs weren't your ordinary, run of the mill frogs. They were special frog that had managed to survive the poisonous waters of their habitat. They didn't look like your average frog either. Some were three legged and others had appendages growing in some pretty awkward places.

The scientists hypothesized that the frogs that survived had undergone mutation in order to stay alive. The poisonous chemicals internally modified their systems thereby increasing the likelihood of their growth and survival.

Those frogs are a constant reminder that there has to be an internal change to help us survive and grow. We may have to make some sacrifices along the way, but the payoff is a new strength we would have never realized if we had not lived through those poisonous times in our lives.

Today, I see growth

_____

_____

_____

_____

_____

_____

_____

_____

_____

_____

_____

_____

_____

Day 5

Very truly, I tell you, unless a grain of wheat falls into the earth and dies, it remains just a single grain; but if it dies, it bears much fruit.

John 12:24 NRSV

Years ago, I received a phone call from a reporter asking for confirmation of a friend's death. It was devastating since I hadn't heard a word prior to the call. Finally, our network of friends gave me the news. How awful! One moment a person is alive and doing what they do and the next they cease to exist.

I prayed for his family's strength. I prayed for his fiancé to have peace of mind. I just prayed. In the midst of one of my prayers, a specific portion of scripture began to echo in my mind; "…unless a grain of wheat falls to the earth and dies…" I opened my Bible to read it in its entirety and was amazed at the peace that swept over my soul. It was the germination process in biblical terms. A seed must shed its external shell and transform in order to expand, bear fruit, and grow.

Sure, we cried and continue to miss that old friend even today, but the peace that came through that revelation of scripture will forever bring me peace as it broadened my understanding of the sacrifices that must be made for growth.

Today, I see growth

_____

_____

_____

_____

_____

_____

_____

_____

_____

_____

_____

_____

_____

_____

Day 6

Beloved, I do not consider that I have made it my own; but this one thing I do: forgetting what lies behind and straining forward to what lies ahead

Philippians 3:13, NRSV

Today, our son graduates from high school. This is an emotional time for me just like it was when he graduated from kindergarten and from the eighth grade. Graduation is an accomplishment that we both worked hard to achieve. However, it can be a bitter-sweet occasion as we celebrate the ending of one thing and the beginning of another.

Our child is leaving high school and about to embark on the next leg of his journey - college. I'm excited as he prepares to move into a new level of independence. I'm also apprehensive as I am thrusted into the position of recreating my own life. Embarking upon these new levels indicates the decision to start over. Starting over means some old things get left behind while some new and different things are embraced. Our son graduating from high school is an accomplishment and a reason to celebrate, but more importantly, it's an opportunity for us both to grow.

Today, I see growth

_____

_____

_____

_____

_____

_____

_____

_____

_____

_____

_____

_____

_____

Day 7

We who are strong ought to put up with the failings of the weak, and not to please ourselves.

Romans 15:1, NRSV

We have a wonderful natural park near our house called the Agricenter International. In one area of the park, they perform field crop research. Every year they plant a field of sunflowers. They are beautiful to look at, but I often wondered if there was a strategy for planting them.

One day, I decided to do some Google research on sunflowers. I learned that some farmers consider them an unwanted weed, but others utilized them for their gift to help other plants grow. Sunflowers have the ability to remove lead and other toxins from ground water and soil. Sunflowers grow to prepare the way for other plants to grow in a healthy environment.

What a wonderful metaphor for those of us in the "Helping Professions." Our purpose is to train, advance, and grow into vehicles that provide healthy environments for others to heal, advance, and grow.

Today, I see growth

_____

_____

_____

_____

_____

_____

_____

_____

_____

_____

_____

_____

_____

_____

Honor

When we honor others, we pay them a great deal of respect and regard. We extend to them actions that show we care in an attempt to nurture who they are as special individuals. We pay honor or tribute to our dead in recognition that their lives impacted ours in some way.

Honor as a key ingredient to deliverance is when we take time out to honor ourselves: our back stories, the pain, the pleasure, and the life lessons gained. We pause and pay tribute to the things we had to leave behind because our past has an impact on our present. This tribute does not involve reliving the past or reminiscing with great sorrow. This tribute is in recognition of the strength we exhibit as the direct result of our journey - our back story.

The best way to honor ourselves is to celebrate who we are. We nurture ourselves by respecting our body, our mind, and our spirit. The key to accomplishing this task is to consider the people, places, and things we expose our bodies, minds, and spirits to. We accomplish this with grace and dignity and not at the expense of another.

For the next seven days, give pause to honor everything that has transpired and created you into the unique gift you are today.

Today, I honor

Day 1

But he said to me, "My grace is sufficient for you, for power is made perfect in weakness."

2 Corinthians 12:9a, NRSV

When our son was young, we attended "A Butterfly Party" held at one of our local landscaping nurseries. It was very informative and of course there were caterpillars for sale and of course we purchased two.

We did everything we were instructed to do and our caterpillars followed the plan. Weeks later, it was time for them to complete their metamorphosis. It was painful to watch as one began to break through its shell. After hours of struggle, I decided to help by gently making the opening a little larger. It seemed to work as our new friend emerged, but when it was time to fly, he seemed awkward. He tried but wasn't able to gain much height. We quickly went to our book to determine what went wrong. To my dismay, I was the source of the problem. The struggle to break free allows a fluid to work its way into the butterfly's wings which strengthens them to fly.

That experience stayed with me. It allowed me to celebrate the fact that I too had been strengthened by many struggles of my past. I honor the conscious decision I made to refuse to remain angry or hurt and I honor the butterfly for the lesson.

Today, I honor

_____

_____

_____

_____

_____

_____

_____

_____

_____

_____

_____

_____

_____

Day 2

Honor your father and your mother, so that your days may be long in the land that the Lord your God is giving you.

Exodus 20:12 NRSV

At the age of twelve, I was molested by my natural father. Deliverance or healing was a very painful and lengthy process but worth the struggle.

It was years after the incident and only a few months after my mother's death, that I noticed a bump in the grieving process. It was difficult getting past anger, but I wasn't clear on who or why I was angry. Finally, one day while journaling, it occurred to me that I was angry at my mother for marrying a man that would do that to his child. I cried and cursed until I was exhausted. Soon afterwards, a sense of peace and calm came over me and I wrote these words, "Dethrone Mama; she did the best she could with what she had."

I had my mother on a throne that imposed the pressure of being and doing everything perfect on her. The truth is she was probably co-dependent and working with dysfunctional relationship tools like many of us are. Seeing my mother through the eyes of a woman and not a daughter helped me to forgive her and forgive myself. Today, I honor my mother for her strength and endurance, and I honor myself for maturity, growth, and acceptance.

Today, I honor

_____

_____

_____

_____

_____

_____

_____

_____

_____

_____

_____

_____

_____

Day 3

*Let marriage be held in honor by all, and let the
marriage bed be kept undefiled; for God will judge
fornicators and adulterers.*

Hebrews 13:4, NRSV

I was young and inexperienced with life the first
time I married. It was a tumultuous relationship, but
it drove me into a relationship with the church and
God. I had to pray to maintain a semblance of
sanity. However, confusion arose when the church
had one thing to say about my marital situation and
God another.

Not understanding that the quiet inner voice that
was leading me to file for divorce was the Spirit of
God, I allowed the louder outside voices to seduce
me into staying nine long years.

Finally, at the fear of losing my mind, I made the
determination that if God was a forgiving God, then
that God would forgive me for divorcing this man.

Months after the divorce, I realized that our vows
stated, "What God has joined together, let no man
put asunder." God didn't do that. I did and I
repented for taking matters into my own hands. To
divorce my first husband was an act of self-care. It
wasn't a dishonorable thing to do - at least not for
me. It was the honorable thing to do.

Today, I honor

_____

_____

_____

_____

_____

_____

_____

_____

_____

_____

_____

_____

_____

Day 4

Or do you not know that your body is a temple of the Holy Spirit within you, which you have from God, and that you are not your own?

1Corinthians 6:19, NRSV

I was thirty-seven years old when I got pregnant with my son. Believe it or not, that was the plan. I didn't want to bring a child into a my first dysfunctional, loveless marriage. The second time I married a man I loved, and we were both committed to the responsibility of parenting.

It was a celebration that started from the time the doctor confirmed I was pregnant. Men were so polite and courteous to me when I was out in public. People were always making things easy for me. I simply loved it, but after I had Dru, the realization was that all of the attention was in honor of the fact that I was carrying new life in me.

My husband pampered me in honor of me carrying his son. People were nice and courteous to me in honor of what pregnancy represents and I honored myself by eating the right foods, eliminating caffeine, walking every day, taking herbs, and on and on. Dru will be nineteen years old by the publishing of this book and I still continue the practice of honoring my body; it's the only one I'll ever have.

Today, I honor

_____

_____

_____

_____

_____

_____

_____

_____

_____

_____

_____

_____

_____

Day 5

*Now therefore perform the doing of it that as there
was a readiness to will, so there may be a
performance also out of that which ye have.*

I Corinthians 8:11 NRSV

I chose to do a project centered on adolescent
behavioral modification for my Doctorate in
Ministry work. While searching for scholarly
resources to support the claim substantiating the
importance of self-esteem, I stumbled upon an
article entitled: *The Pursuit of Self-Esteem:
Contingencies of Self-Worth and Self-Regulation*
written by J. Crocker, A. T. Brook, Yu Niiya, and
M. Villacorta all from the University of Michigan.

They described self-esteem as the characteristic that
fluctuates with successes and failures. However,
according to the findings shared in this article, self-
regulation is when an individual will put forth the
effort to accomplish their goals while considering
any level of failure as an opportunity to learn. Self-
regulation helps us identify our weaknesses, so they
can be addressed and an alternative plan devised.
That information stuck with me as it gave me the
right to honor my struggles, setbacks, missed
opportunities, and outright failures for the
information each of them gave me. Today, I
practice self-regulation as it allows me to honor my
past and see all the bumps in my life as stepping
stones.

Today, I honor

Day 6

Do not judge, and you will not be judged; do not condemn, and you will not be condemned. Forgive, and you will be forgiven

Luke 6:37 NRSV

I've shared the tragic details of being molested to hundreds of people. Forgiving and forgetting is hard work. I'll never forget, but I eventually learned to forgive.

The incident with my father was safely tucked away in the basement of my mind until I married my first husband. One night, when we were about to make love, scenes of that horrid day began to flash through my mind. For years I prayed, went to therapy, journaled, and eventually allowed the entire scene to play itself out in my mind. It hurt. I felt dirty, but somehow I robbed those memories of the fear and pain they once held over me. These were only the first steps and they took twenty years to accomplish.

Next, I wrote a letter to my father explaining how I remember what he did, didn't understand why he did it but was willing to move forward and try to forgive him. This took another five years. Finally, at his bed side over thirty years later, I was able to forgive him and let go of the pain of my past.

It wasn't easy and there were no short cuts, but today I honor myself for having the courage to do so and I honor anyone who attempts to do the same.

Today, I honor

Day 7

When those who were around him saw what was coming, they asked, "Lord, should we strike with the sword?" Then one of them struck the slave of the high priest and cut off his right ear But Jesus said, "No more of this!" And he touched his ear and healed him.

Luke 22:49-51 NRSV

In preparing a sermon, I considered the term "fight or flight." It's a reference to the automatic response that our bodies take in the presence of a real or imagined threat.

However, I decided to reflect on the words alone and not just the theory. I thought about various situations and obstacles I had encountered since accepting the call to ministry. Each time, I had to make a choice whether to stand and fight the powers that be or take flight by turning, walking away, and removing myself from the situation at hand.

An over inflated ego and out of balanced pride will place layers of guilt and shame on us for deciding to take flight and remove ourselves from unfavorable situations. Today, I honor every time I made the decision to take flight and remove myself from situations and people that might have otherwise cause me to act or say something foolishly in an attempt to win a battle I had no business fighting.

Today, I honor

Integrate

The first time I baked a cake from scratch was a scary task. A client had passed on to me her mothers' recipe for homemade butter pound cake. While reading over the recipe, I noticed only solid ingredients and no liquids. Being the novice baker that I was, I asked if I was to add milk? The answer was an astounding "NO!" So I bought everything I needed to bake my first cake from scratch.

It was a practice in discipline to follow the recipe and not add milk. The ingredients didn't seem like they were meant to blend without the aid of a liquid. Butter, flour, eggs, and sugar were clumped in the mixing bowl like wads of gunk. I remember how adamant she was that I didn't stray from the recipe, so I kept stirring and mixing in hopes of eventually accomplishing a smooth batter.

Minutes later, what appeared to be a hopeless situation evolved into the smooth batter of a professional baker and finally a wonderful dessert. The lesson I learned that day and will always remember is sometimes things that don't seem to integrate will come together and blend if we are patient and stick with the process.

The next seven days are dedicated to a time of integration. Reflect over all of the principles you've learned thus far and find a way to combine them into your daily routine and way of life. Take time and integrate for renewal and a fresh start.

Today, I will work to integrate

_____

_____

_____

_____

_____

_____

_____

_____

_____

_____

_____

_____

_____

Day 1

Because you know that the testing of your faith produces endurance; and let endurance have its full effect, so that you may be mature and complete, lacking in nothing.

James 1:3-4, NRSV

Dru has tried his hand in lots of sports: little league football, junior soccer, and finally basketball. Once he became interested in basketball, he went to great lengths to master the game. He watched YouTube videos of player after player to observe their moves. Then he would practice outside and at the gym for hours to perfect and develop his own signature moves.

Finally, one day he came in after a hard practice session and declared, "I need to jump higher." As the encouraging mom I try to be, I reassured him that he was on the right path. Keep watching how the greats do it, practice, eat right, hydrate often, take your vitamins, and believe. He looked at me like surely there was more to it than that. It was as though he thought there was a "jump high" trick he wasn't made aware of.

The truth of his matter and ours is that if we consistently practice the simple things and integrate them with healthier choices and belief in our abilities, we will all jump higher.

Today, I will work to integrate

_____

_____

_____

_____

_____

_____

_____

_____

_____

_____

_____

_____

_____

_____

Day 2

From whom the whole body, joined and knit together by every ligament with which it is equipped, as each part is working properly, promotes the body's growth in building itself up in love.

Ephesians 4:16 NRSV

My play sister owns thirteen dogs, two cats, and a missing bird. Sounds like one of cats went AWOL. She rescued them and when she ran out of room, we rescued one. One day, she offered us a little, wild-haired Fox Terrier, whom my son named Garry.

We were excited about our new family pet. However, our Labrador retriever, Spot, didn't share our joy. The trick to integrating Garry into our pack was to make sure Spot felt like he was the top dog. Besides, he was our only pet for almost eight years. That could spoil a dog. Spot was fed first at feeding times. Spot was brushed first. We would put the lease on Spot first, then Garry. We wanted Spot to know he was still special while integrating Garry into our routine. Spot needed to know we weren't replacing him and Garry needed to feel loved and safe. Today, we are one big happy family.

There is an art to incorporating new pets, people, and even ideas into a system that has been the same for so long. Nevertheless, everyone benefits when it is strategically done.

Today, I will work to integrate

_____

_____

_____

_____

_____

_____

_____

_____

_____

_____

_____

_____

_____

Day 3

Hatred stirs up strife, but love covers all offenses.

Proverbs 10:12 NRSV

After the messy divorce from my first husband, I lived alone. It was scary at times, but I wanted to learn to live and love myself again.

One night, I heard noises in the backyard. I went to the den to get a good view. There was a pack of dogs. I went out to see what drew them into the yard, and there was this scared, beautiful English Spaniel trapped by a herd of dogs. I shewed them away, comforted the Spaniel, and returned to bed. Early the next morning, I heard a scratching sound at the front door. I opened the door and that same Spaniel ran into my house and to the back door. I opened the back door and she made her home in my back yard. I looked at her collar and there was an updated license but no owners' information. So I put notices of a "found dog" around the neighborhood. Meanwhile, we grew closer as I cared for her. After a month, I decided to take her to the Vet to make sure she wasn't sick and learned she was pregnant.

Not long afterwards, my house was filled with twelve adorable puppies. No one ever claimed my new friend, I named Sheba. We took care of each other until she was too old and too sick to live on. Sheba was integrated into my life when I was afraid to trust love and for that I'm eternally grateful.

Today, I will work to integrate

_____

_____

_____

_____

_____

_____

_____

_____

_____

_____

_____

_____

_____

Day 4

Please pay no attention, my lord, to that wicked man Nabal. He is just like his name—his name means Fool, and folly goes with him. And as for me, your servant, I did not see the men my lord sent.

1 Samuel 25:25 NRSV

We started planning for our new arrival the moment we learned I was pregnant. My husband and I would visit bookstores and read books about *What to Expect When You're Expecting* and look for hours through books of baby names and their meanings. We both agreed that we wanted to select a name that meant something, a name that would serve as a description and a prophecy.

My brother suggested naming a boy child after him. Of course that was out of the question, but we agreed to integrate his middle name if we had a boy and my middle name if we had a girl. Meanwhile, we searched for meaningful genderless names. We finally stumbled upon the name Dru/Drew. It was perfect, genderless and meaningful. The name Dru/Drew means "wise one, loved one, warrior."

June 30, 1997 we gave birth to a 7 pound, 11 ounce baby boy. His name is Dru (Wise one) Vincent (Conquering one) Bernard (Brave as a bear). His name represents the integration of both of our family's lineage and I see him growing into the fullness of his name daily.

Today, I will work to integrate

_____

_____

_____

_____

_____

_____

_____

_____

_____

_____

_____

_____

_____

_____

Day 5

For it was you who formed my inward parts; you knit me together in my mother's womb. I praise you, for I am fearfully and wonderfully made. Wonderful are your works; that I know very well

Psalm 139:13-14 NRSV

I am a lifelong learner, which has afforded me career opportunities as a hairstylist, fashion merchandiser, certified life coach, spiritual director, real estate agent, ordained minister, and addiction counselor.

When I would change hair styles or get another degree or certification, people would say, "You just don't know what you want to do with yourself, do you?" My response would always be a resounding, "Of course I do and it's all of the above." There may appear to be a disconnection between each of my careers, but every one of them supports the next. Integration has been the key.

The skills I learned as a life coach have empowered me to work with and really be present with others. As an ordained minister and addiction counselor, I have learned how to appreciate the gift of life and love.

What others may see as a fragmented individual that operates in various departments is a fully matured, integrated woman that is equipped to serve others. Don't be afraid to integrate all of who you are and what you love.

Today, I will work to integrate

_____

_____

_____

_____

_____

_____

_____

_____

_____

_____

_____

_____

_____

_____

_____

Day 6

Therefore, what God has joined together, let no one separate.

Mark 10:9 NRSV

Our pet dog raised our son. My husband was concerned about having our pet dog in the house after the baby was born. He didn't grow up with an actual pet and after a couple of run-ins with some neighborhood dogs, he became a little anxious about having pets around.

Not me, I've always loved animals and was fortunate enough to have owned a variety of pets over my lifetime. I wasn't the least bit worried about how the new baby would be received by our pet Spaniel Sheba. While lying on the couch or floor, Sheba would just sniff around my stomach. She started to make this a daily practice. It was like she was keeping tabs on the baby, making sure everything was okay.

After Dru was born, my husband came to accept that Sheba was the perfect babysitter. She would lay right by his play pen and watch his every move. They became the very best of friends.

The same can be true when we experience considerable changes in our lives. Plan for it, work towards it, and watch how acceptance and integration will make transition that much easier.

Today, I will work to integrate

_____

_____

_____

_____

_____

_____

_____

_____

_____

_____

_____

_____

_____

_____

Day 7

He who forms the mountains, who creates the wind, and who reveals his thoughts to mankind, who turns dawn to darkness, and treads on the heights of the earth the Lord God Almighty is his name.

Amos 4:13 NRSV

I am an eclectic minister called to ministry through the rhythmic sounds of a spoken word piece.

One day while sitting and enjoying the autumn breeze, I closed my eyes and allowed the wind to relax my racing thoughts. Suddenly but quietly, I began to hear these words, "My people don't know me..." I immediately wrote them down to see if I'd gain greater understanding and my pen wouldn't stop. It was amazing, unreal, and spiritual. Afterwards, I read aloud what was written and somehow knew this was the explanation of my purpose.

That experience taught me a vital lesson that I continue to live by and that is, God is in everything. In many ways, religion has taught us to separate God from certain aspects of our lives but this is a call to integrate for some and reintegrate for others, God back into every area of our lives and realize where our true passions lie.

Today, I will work to integrate

Juxtapose

In seminary, the language of the natives can best be described as an Ebonics version of biblical English with Greek and Latin undertones. I didn't understand half of what I read and very little of what I heard. The word that helped transition me into this world of new beginnings was "Juxtaposition."

I allowed myself to be tormented by the repetitive use of this word in multiple texts before searching for a definition, only to be amazed by the simplicity of its meaning. Juxtapose is defined as laying side by side as in determining pros and cons. It is a type of comparison and contrast. This is the seventh principle to help guide us through the processes of our lives.

Consider our earth's seasonal nature as a metaphor to describe the processes of life. There are times in everyone's life when pruning and purging is necessary. Decisions have to be made, people change, places undergo transformation, and sometimes we outgrow things.

Use the next seven days to juxtapose the various decisions, people, places, and things to help determine what's vital to your healing and sanity and what's not. It's all a part of the process.

Today, I juxtapose the following for clarity

Day 1

Then Peter began to speak to them: "I truly understand that God shows no partiality, but in every nation anyone who fears him and does what is right is acceptable to him

Acts 10:34-35 NRSV

I was so horribly angry with God. Here I am, once again, husbandless, jobless, and confused.

Days turned into weeks which evolved into months that dissolved into years of prayer, looking for answers, in search of what went wrong. How could someone dedicated to prayer not have her prayers answered?

Hence, down the street I stomp accusing God of being unfair. Suddenly, I heard these words, "I never said I was fair; life isn't fair, but I am just." Looking at these two words side by side, they appear to be synonymous. However, as I continued to reflect and pray concerning the words I had heard, a realization came through. Skin for skin or an eye for an eye is fair, but justice points to what is morally right. Juxtaposing those words helped me to understand what I heard. Life does not always give us what we deserve and sometimes that works in our favor, but we can always expect God to point us in the direction of what is morally right.

Today, I juxtapose the following for clarity

_____

_____

_____

_____

_____

_____

_____

_____

_____

_____

_____

_____

_____

_____

Day 2

For now we see in a mirror, dimly, but then we will see face to face. Now I know only in part; then I will know fully, even as I have been fully known.

1Corinthians 13:12 NRSV

Dirty secrets in the email. That is how I learned my husband was having an affair. Reading those words felt like an out of body experience. Time became elusive. All feeling left my body as my thoughts began to search for answers to questions that weren't even formed.

Suddenly, it hit me like a fist to the chest, and I took a breath and began to cry. It was uncontrollable. I couldn't stop it. The ache in my chest would not go away. This felt like someone had died. When I considered the situation, it was clear that something had died. Extramarital affairs are betrayal and betrayal is death. Unconditional trust had died.

They say it is better to have loved and lost then to never have loved at all. Losing love hurts, but while journaling my thoughts, it became clear that this pain was in direct comparison to the depth of love we had. Life happens to us all and some of us deal with it in less favorable ways, but when you juxtapose the good alongside the bad, use the evidence to make you better and grateful.

Today, I juxtapose the following for clarity

_____

_____

_____

_____

_____

_____

_____

_____

_____

_____

_____

_____

_____

_____

Day 3

Love is patient; love is kind; love is not envious or boastful or arrogant or rude. It does not insist on its own way; it is not irritable or resentful;

1 Corinthians 13:4-5 NRSV

My first husband was addicted to crack cocaine. Those nine years of marriage were turbulent. Divorce crossed my mind when we approached our fourth anniversary. However, my reluctance to look at the entire equation kept me in that hell-hole an additional five years.

Finally, one day I stood in the window gazing over our backyard in despair. A decision had to be made. Do I go or do I stay? Do I risk my sanity and stay in this impaired mess of a marriage or do I cut my losses and go? Is it more important to have a husband or to have peace? Is this love or some type of sick devotion?

The decision to leave was not an easy one. In many ways it felt like failure, but after careful consideration the answers were clear. By juxtaposing leaving alongside of staying, it was obvious that our relationship was not built on love and mutual respect but something dysfunctional and debilitating. It was a gift to consider all the aspects and an even greater gift to be able to walk away and be free.

Today, I juxtapose the following for clarity

_____

_____

_____

_____

_____

_____

_____

_____

_____

_____

_____

_____

_____

_____

Day 4

*We know that all things work together for good for
those who love God, who are called according to
his purpose.*

Romans 8:28 NRSV

110 degrees is normal for a Memphis summer day.
With temperatures like these, it pays to keep a good
HVAC person as a friend.

When our friend Carlos came by the house to give
our units a good cleaning and once-over, I never
thought I'd learn a life lesson. He took his time with
the outside units and cleaned them inside and out.
He measured Freon and hooked up gauges to do
things I never imagined. After what seemed to be a
couple of hours, he came inside and asked where
the furnace was located. While directing him to the
attic, I explained that for financial reasons I would
wait on cleaning the furnaces. Carlos kept moving
towards the attic as he explained that they both
work together.

A lesson sprung out of those words as they
repeatedly danced in my head. Hot and cold, winter
and summer, Ying and Yang work together to
provide us with comfort, growth, and balance. It's a
revelation worth considering. Juxtapose the people,
places, things, and events in your life and see the
harmony of opposites working for our good.

Today, I juxtapose the following for clarity

_____

_____

_____

_____

_____

_____

_____

_____

_____

_____

_____

_____

_____

_____

Day 5

Suppose one of you wants to build a tower. Won't you first sit down and estimate the cost to see if you have enough money to complete it?

Luke 14:28 NRSV

Writing away stress is a tactical maneuver I learned at the age of ten. It started with me keeping a daily record of my thoughts in a little pocket diary my mother had given me. I loved that little book with the lock and key. It quickly became my safe place.

Eventually, I grew out of this practice. My peers went out for drinks, got high, and smoked cigarettes when things got stressful. Not wanting to be the school nerd, I did the same. I was a full blown addict by the time I was half way through college and not in any position to manage stress.

One day, out of pure frustration, I started randomly writing. By the time the page was full, I felt a sense of relief I had not known for years. Writing without fear of criticism or judgment helped me to weigh the variables and juxtapose the concerns. This allowed me to determine the best strategy for my life. Today, the practice of journaling continues to be an intricate part of my reflection and devotion. It has helped me make the best decisions for my overall well-being.

Today, I juxtapose the following for clarity

_____

_____

_____

_____

_____

_____

_____

_____

_____

_____

_____

_____

_____

_____

Day 6

*I call heaven and earth to witness against you
today that I have set before you life and death,
blessings and curses. Choose life so that you and
your descendants may live...*

Deuteronomy 30:19 NRSV

Stand up and fight for what you want or turn and
take flight from your present circumstances. That
was the decision to be made at the onslaught of
launching Spirit Builders. I began to unintentionally
juxtapose the variables for clarity while jotting
down my thoughts. The following is a portion of
what I wrote:

Which way do I go? Who should I see? What do I
do? Will someone help me? Who should I work
with? Where should I live? Who do I trust? How
much should I give? Is this it or did I miss that? Do
I trust Karma or search for the facts? Which way do
I go? What should I do? Do I do it alone or work
with you?

Do I file for a grant or apply for a loan? Do I work
from an office or do I work from home? So what do
I do, where do I go? Do I continue to trust God?
Yes, Sir, and then some more…

Juxtaposition even in poetic verse yields the same
results. Clarity.

Today, I juxtapose the following for clarity

Day 7

*And will not God grant justice to his chosen ones
who cry to him day and night? Will he delay long in
helping them?*

Luke 18:7 NRSV

Life ain't fair and neither is God. Every morning, I
would walk the streets of our subdivision and
proceed to tell God, "It's not fair that men are
accepted in ministry more readily then women.
God, it's not fair how people of little integrity
always close the bigger deals. It's not fair, Lord,
how whorish women can tear a family a part and
live happily ever after. It's not fair how men grow
tired and leave and women are left holding the bag
with the children and mortgage in it. Life just ain't
fair."

One day as I turned the corner, a gust of air took my
breath and I heard these words: "I never said I was
fair, but I am just." Before this instance, I thought
the two words had the same meaning. Although in
some regard they are synonymous, they differ in
other respects. "Fair" means "in accordance with
the rules" as an adjective and "without cheating" as
an adverb. However, "just" as an adjective means
"according to what is morally right" while as an
adverb it means "exactly."

After juxtaposing the definitions of "fair" and
"just," I thanked God for being "exactly" where I'm
supposed to be and that includes living out the
design God has for my life.

Today, I juxtapose the following for clarity

_____

_____

_____

_____

_____

_____

_____

_____

_____

_____

_____

_____

_____

_____

Kindle

My first job was at a neighborhood barber shop where the owner would burn split ends off his client's hair. It was a dramatic display that kept the shop busy six days a week.

Although clients were always amazed at the show. Someone would always ask "why?" The answer is quite simple as burning hair is an old approach to removing dead ends. I'm sure the practice was stopped because hair burns quickly (a type of purifying practice) and that makes it a dangerous practice.

As we continue through the process of deliverance, we discover the power of our stories. Although we have heard it before, it comes to life as we welcome the experience. We are the easily ignited pieces that can set our world around us on fire. When we share our experiences and how we were able to weather the process of deliverance, it will ignite a fresh determination that will help others to forge through their own process. That's when the purification process is at its best - cleaning up dead weight for both parties because the kindling doesn't stop burning as it ignites the things that come into contact with it; it continues to burn, shine, and render warmth for all around.

Approach the next seven days with an eagerness to share your story and watch the world around you catch on fire.

Today, I will

_____

_____

_____

_____

_____

_____

_____

_____

_____

_____

_____

_____

_____

_____

Day 1

I came to the exiles at Tel-abib, who lived by the river Chebar. And I sat there among them, stunned, for seven days.

Ezekiel 3:14 NRSV

I worried about how effective I would be in ministry after my husband decided he didn't want a life with me and our child any longer. What would people think about a prayer warrior that couldn't keep her happy home happy and together?

Then as I was considering accounts throughout my life that would help illustrate this tenth principle, kindle, I recognized the power that could and would resonate from my story if I worked through each principle and fully embraced the lessons therein. My story, this story would ignite the burning fire of life and strengthen others that felt abandoned, unloved, wounded, and alone.

This is where I am literally today, in a place where I have made enough steps to be able to share my story. This story was years in the making because it took me years to come successfully to this point in my life. This story has the power to ignite you because it comes with the experience of sitting right where some of you find yourself sitting today. When I got up from that place and started this process, I walked away stronger than I've ever been before.

Today, I will

Day 2

A little yeast leavens the whole batch of dough.

Galatians 5:9 NRSV

Our son loves fashion forward casually chic clothes with a beach bum appeal. When he returned from a youth retreat in Palm Beach, Florida, he found a new love in a line of clothing called Vineyard Vines. Like any fashionable mom, I Googled the store's location and off we went.

While in the store, Dru enjoyed shopping while I was intrigued by the behind the scenes story. It started when two friends decided to quit their desk jobs and spend more time at Martha's Vineyard on their boat fishing and just doing the things that make them happy. When funds got low, they started to sell ties they designed with themes from their favored surroundings and the rest is a story of continued success.

Their story added fuel to an ember concerning starting a business my son had but couldn't find the motivation to get the ball rolling. The fiery passion of their story stirred the embers of our son's fire and now he is a blazing inferno ready to launch his vision. And to think it all started with the kindle of someone else's fire.

Today, I will

_____

_____

_____

_____

_____

_____

_____

_____

_____

_____

_____

_____

_____

Day 3

But they have conquered him by the blood of the Lamb and by the word of their testimony, for they did not cling to life even in the face of death.

Revelation 12:11 NRSV

I tried to get my husband sober by going to Al-Anon and AA meetings. The lesson learned was I am just as sick as he was if I thought there was anything I could do to make him stop drinking and using.

Through it all, I became quite attached to those twelve step meetings and my focused shifted from trying to get him sober to working on finding my authentic self.

Each meeting was more inspiring than the one before. I tried several of them, AA, NA, and CA. Each one of them brought similar results because at each and every meeting someone would share their experience, strength, and hope. This is the corner stone of the AA meeting; every one gives back through service work and sharing their story in hopes that someone will hear and accept the challenge of recovery. Today, I am proud to be numbered among the millions of recovering people who share their experiences to help others know they are not alone. Recovering people work like kindle does to a fire. It's a way of life.

Today, I will

Day 4

*But who can endure the day of his coming, and who
can stand when he appears? For he is like a
refiner's fire and like fullers' soap;*

Malachi 3:2 NRSV

I watched my Uncle Charlie slaughter a whole hog
one day. I was intrigued until he split that giant
caucus of an animal from his throat straight down
the middle of his belly and what appeared to be
miles of tubing fell out. As that grey matter laid in
the grass and look like small waves shifting back
and forth, I asked Uncle Charley, "What is that?"
He looked up with a smile and took that hunter's
knife and started to split that tubing open to reveal a
sight and smell that stopped my chitterling eating
days right in their tracks.

Slaughtering that hog was an all-day event as Aunt
Jennie would wash and boil great slabs of meat to
prepare for the grill. Periodically, she would look up
and give me instructions, as if there was some threat
of me ever having to repeat this practice when I
grew older. "You got to make sure the fire is at the
right temperature to purify this meat or else you
may get worms. The right amount of heat will just
about kill any impurity."

That's how effective sharing our story is; it's the
right amount of heat to get a good fire going to
purify the soul. That's' show we gain clarity.

Today, I will

_____

_____

_____

_____

_____

_____

_____

_____

_____

_____

_____

_____

_____

Day 5

And he said to them, "Go into all the world and proclaim the good news to the whole creation."

Mark 16:15 NRSV

I started working in a popular neighborhood barber shop at the age of seventeen. I was virtually unknown, nervous, and without a clientele. After weeks of sitting around, I noticed that the typical client that frequent the establishment was a businessman that got the works: haircut, shampoo, and shave. No one trusted me yet to cut and shave, but I decided to offer an add on services that would help the master barbers get more clients done per hour, allow our clients to feel special, and provide me an income. I would do the shampoo and facial cleansing while the barbers started on the next client. By the time they were finished with the next cut, I would have their previous client prepped for their shave. Before I knew it, I had clients asking specifically for my services without ever paying for an ad. The clients had spread the word to their friends and family and my clientele flourished as the result of it.

That's exactly how the good news of your story will affect those around you. Everyone loves to be a part of something that makes them feel good; it brightens our perspective and makes us want to spread the joy.

Today, I will

Day 6

The tongue has the power of life and death, and those who love it will eat its fruit.

Proverbs 18:21 NRSV

One day I walked into a full-fledged war when I entered the office. The air was so tensed that it could be cut with a knife. As soon as I entered my work space, the clients began to pour in. One by one, they came and cried and told their version of the weekend's events.

Client A was seen by Client B as she went through Client C's belongings. So Client B told Client D what she thought she saw and D told E and so on until the news got to Client G who took matters into her own hands and went to clients B, D, E, and F to share her view on thieves of which she felt Client A was one. Meanwhile Client A was devastated by the fact that everyone seemed to be whispering and glaring at her when she came into the room. Her only friend was Client C, who had not been approached with the gossip and who originally told Client A to go and get some candy earlier from her bag.

It took several private sessions and the better part of an eight hour shift to unravel the lies, but the truth brought a sweet sigh of peace that rekindled friendships. You can stop the spread of foolishness and kindle some hope by sharing the truth.

Today, I will

Day 7

So neither the one who plants nor the one who waters is anything, but only God who gives the growth.

I Corinthians 3:7 NRSV

If I told you the chicken dipped snuff, then look under the wings. As eccentric as it sounds, this was a motto I lived by.

I discovered the power of my story immediately after starting full-time ministry and looked for every opportunity to share it with other struggling brothers and sisters in despair. Early disillusionment set in as I struggled with the question, "Why would anyone choose to go through something when they are offered a better alternative?" I became impatient with those I served as they appeared to intentionally do the things that we warned them were not in their best interest. Eventually, I got fed up and decided that sharing my story in hopes of helping others was a waste of my time. People were going to do what they wanted to do when they wanted to do it no matter how foolish the decision.

As the universe would have it, I was brought out of my stupor after hearing the story of a pastor that had struggled with some of the same thoughts and feelings I was experiencing. In one full sweep of events, I was both inspired and my faith renewed in the power of our stories.

Today, I will

Love

Love is a many splendored thing. That was the first line of one of our most popular Glee Club songs from my junior high school days. I didn't think much about what we were singing back in those days, but time truly does bring about a change.

How often have you pondered over the question of love? Love is a concept that we have metaphors, songs, poems, and various other descriptions for but no real definition. It could possibly be because love is a many splendored thing. It is great and grand, brilliant and gorgeous, it is magnificent. Love is an adjective and a verb. It describes a feeling to be experienced and an action to be taken. Love is intentional living, intentional laughing, and purposely giving of ourselves.

As we entered our final week of working through the principles of the deliverance process, we reflect on how to incorporate making the commitment to live, laugh, and love daily. This is a vital piece to our recovery. When we live intentional and when we laugh out loud, we spread the love we have for self, life, and God.

Let this week be an experience in the splendor of love.

Today, I will

_____

_____

_____

_____

_____

_____

_____

_____

_____

_____

_____

_____

_____

Day 1

When they had finished breakfast, Jesus said to Simon Peter, 'Simon son of John, do you love me more than these?' He said to him, 'Yes, Lord; you know that I love you.' Jesus said to him, 'Feed my lambs.'

John 21:15 NRSV

Ice Cream is my drug of choice. It is the one thing that numbs all pain. After a stressful day, I maybe too tired to eat but never too tired for ice cream. If I yield to temptation and start eating the first spoonful, all anxiety begins to leave my body and instantly my thoughts become crystal clear. Eventually, the realization came that ice cream was like a narcotic to my system. This may not appear to be a bad thing, especially since ice cream appears to be a far cry from drugs or alcohol. However, the calories, the carbs, the fat, the sugar, and the very idea of giving over power to anything other than my Higher Power was a sign of personal neglect and disrespect for my body.

When we learn to live and love intentionally, we'll embrace the idea of balance and we will fall in love with ourselves and start caring for our bodies. I still like ice cream, but I no longer require it to soothe my anxieties. I have God to help me with that.

Today, I will

Day 2

A cheerful heart is a good medicine, but a downcast spirit dries up the bones.

Proverbs 17:22 NRSV

I invested nine hard years into an abusive, dysfunctional marriage where addiction was the glue that kept us together. His drug of choice may have been cocaine but mine was him. I was addicted to having a companion and to the drama-filled life we lived. I was afraid to be alone with myself and of hearing my own thoughts. So I stayed in that loveless relationship in an effort to feel good about me. Begging, pleading, manipulating, justifying, hiding, and rescuing were descriptions of my full-time job as an enabler.

One day, a force greater then myself, gave me the sense and strength enough to leave and never look back. After the reality of my decision kicked in, I was devastated. Today, I realize that the devastation I felt were detox symptoms associated with my drug of choice. I was lonely and afraid of being alone. But as I worked at accepting and loving myself, the alone times were rarely lonely times. There were a few times where I relapsed along the way. However, today I am a person in recovery, learning to live, laugh and enjoy life…one day at a time.

Today, I will

_____

_____

_____

_____

_____

_____

_____

_____

_____

_____

_____

_____

_____

_____

Day 3

Therefore, since we are surrounded by so great a cloud of witnesses, let us also lay aside every weight and the sin that clings so closely, and let us run with perseverance the race that is set before us

Hebrews 12: 1NRSV

All men leave. That was the conclusion one of my clients came to after watching her father leave her mother for another woman and boyfriend after boyfriend doing the same. Her words stabbed me straight through the heart as I realized that although our stories were different, our belief systems were built on very similar foundations - a lot of men leave.

Professionally, I came to accept this dilemma as a by-product of generational conditioning where dysfunction continues to swallow up love, respect, and commitment. However, personally, I struggled to keep dysfunction from destroying my own faith in love. Faith breeds hope, expectation, and a commitment to approach life from a fresh perspective daily. Then the challenge becomes one of reaching out and helping others refocus. The more we rehearse situations and circumstances that bruised and battered us, the more we attract the same. Refocusing involves making a personal commitment to intentionally change to live and laugh and love… again.

Today, I will

Day 4

Beloved, I do not consider that I have made it my own; but this one thing I do: forgetting what lies behind and straining forward to what lies ahead...

Philippians 3:13, NRSV

Carol had a boyfriend for every day of the week. She was fresh out of a nasty divorce and ready to numb the pain of any past memories with work-filled days and party-filled nights. She managed to keep this pace going for several years before her heart felt desires for love, commitment, and a family began to emerge again.

When the ladies would get together, she would start complaining about how she was too old to start a family and didn't have the energy or time to locate a good man. Soon, the change began. We heard transition in her voice, in her plans, and in the very fact that she was considering giving up six of her boyfriends to spend time with one. It was a bold, brave move full of apprehension, but she made it. She was able to navigate all of her fears and reservations into what is a loving, committed relationship today, complete with fulfilling days and nights.

The lesson the rest of us ladies learned from Carol was that it's important to move through our fears if we sincerely desire change. If we choose to do so, everything becomes a possibility.

Today, I will

_____

_____

_____

_____

_____

_____

_____

_____

_____

_____

_____

_____

_____

_____

Day 5

*And now faith, hope, and love abide, these three;
and the greatest of these is love.*

1Corinthians 13:13, NRSV

Dana got pregnant in high school. She was so
ashamed and afraid to see the disappointment in her
mother's face until she managed to hide it for nine
months. The day finally came when it was time to
deliver and Dana's mom was hit with the double
whammy of pregnancy and childbirth with one cool
blow. Seeing her new grandchild softened her heart
to the degree that very little was said of the
circumstances that brought her into this world. They
all returned home and her mother raised both her
and her daughter to the degree that Dana felt like
they were siblings.

Like siblings, Dana began to resent her daughter for
getting the love and attention she never had. One
day, Dana received a call that her mother had been
hospitalized after having a severe stroke. She was in
the hospital for months recovering. Dana was left
alone to care for her daughter who she had grown to
despise. One day, the little girl came up to Dana,
afraid, confused, and asking why her grand-gram
wasn't coming home. She climbed into her mother's
lap and held her neck tight and cried. Suddenly,
Dana felt something surge through her mid-section
and into her chest she'd never felt before. It was
love, innocent unconditional love. This was the day
Dana started to live again. This was the day she
relearned how to love.

Today, I will

_____

_____

_____

_____

_____

_____

_____

_____

_____

_____

_____

_____

_____

_____

Day 6

*I press on toward the goal for the prize of the
heavenly call of God in Christ Jesus.*

Philippians 3:14, NRSV

After Jennie's husband left, she started on this quest
to find out why. Painstakingly, she listed her
character defects. She made the commitment to do
whatever it took to shape her behavior for the better
in hopes of avoiding any future break-ups.

One day, she was driving to work and listening to a
morning talk show. The topic was discipline. She
reached to turn the volume up so she could learn
more on the topic . Much to her surprise, her
thoughts turned to her ex-husband and an Ah-Ha
moment was born.

Jennie learned that commitment takes discipline,
discipline of character. Love requires commitment
which requires discipline. Why do we expect
undisciplined people to discipline themselves and
commit to a long-term relationship? The answer lies
in that question. The answer is commitment.
Sticking and staying is the cure to a lack of
discipline and the remedy for learning how to
commit.

Make the commitment to be the best you can be,
living the best life available - not as revenge or in
retaliation of what others may have done but
because you are learning the discipline of loving
yourself.

Today, I will

Day 7

Peace I leave with you; my peace I give to you. I do not give to you as the world gives. Do not let your hearts be troubled, and do not let them be afraid.

John 14:27, NRSV

Night after night of clinched teeth, tossing and turning, following days of insatiable hunger and irritability, eventually made Yvonne seek professional help. Once at the doctor and after several tests, the doctor came into the examination room and sat down. He started an inquisition that seemed to have no relevancy to her complaints. What did her response to inconsiderate drivers cutting in line have to do with her appetite? However, she trusted her doctor which led her to accept his diagnosis of situational anxiety disorder. Yvonne expected several prescriptions, but the doctor took a different approach and advised her to take some time off and relax.

She reluctantly followed his advice and drove to Gulf Shores for three days of R & R. The first day just about drove her crazy as she sat on the beach trying to think of things to do to relax. It was the end of the second day that she noticed some people in the water playing volleyball. They laughed as they struggled against the incoming waves to remain standing. She heard the laughter amidst the rushing sounds of the waves and became lost in the experience for hours. It was as if the sights and sounds from that scene had hypnotized her. The change in temperature as the sun began to set was the only thing that broke the trance.

As she walked back to the hotel, she felt like she was gliding, but quickly brushed off the feeling believing she was light-headed from being out in the sun all day. So she decided to take a cool shower to lower her body temp.

She carefully slathered lotion over her entire body after drying off and suddenly noticed her unpolished toes. So she pulled out her supplies and took the time to shape and polish them. Then she went onto the balcony to allow her freshly painted toes to dry and found herself watching the boats as they docked. Again, the change in temperature broke the trance as the coolness of the night air began to blow in. She realized several hours had passed. Reflecting over the days' events, Yvonne found that although she hadn't been busy, she hadn't been bored or felt lonely either.

Continuing to feel drunk from relaxation, she retired for the night. She woke up to the warmth of the morning sun and the sound of honking sea gulls. She got up feeling ten pounds lighter. A smile stretched across her face as she realized that this experience was healing.

Hopefully, as we come to the end of this leg of our journey, you each feel a sense of healing and empowerment much like our friend Yvonne. Remember to make a commitment to embrace each of these twelve principles and incorporate them into your everyday life.

Embracing these principles means to live through them and refer to them daily. By doing so, you will find endurance to conquer any process.

For this week and hopefully for the balance of your lives, make the commitment to live, love, and laugh.

Today, I will

_____

_____

_____

_____

_____

_____

_____

_____

_____

_____

_____

Now I am ready to make the commitment to

_____

_____

_____

_____

_____

_____

_____

_____

_____

_____

_____

_____

_____

Made in United States
Orlando, FL
30 August 2023

36561453R00121